The LIE of the GOOD LIFE

Fifty Women Tell the Truth

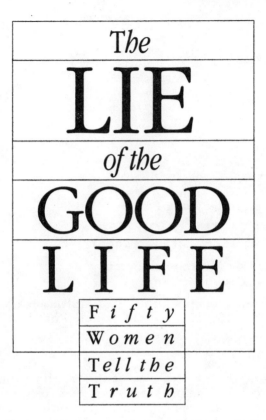

Alice Slaikeu Lawhead

MULTNOMAH

Portland Oregon 97266

Cover design by Kreig Barrie

THE LIE OF THE GOOD LIFE
© 1989 by Alice Slaikeu Lawhead

Published by Multnomah Press
Portland, Oregon 97266

Multnomah Press is a ministry of Multnomah School of
the Bible, 8435 N.E. Glisan Street, Portland, Oregon
97220

Printed in U.S.A.

Library of Congress Cataloging-in-Publication Data

Lawhead, Alice.
    The lie of the good life: fifty women tell the truth/Alice
Slaikeu Lawhead.
      p. cm.
    ISBN 0-88070-315-6
    1. Women in Christianity—United States. 2. Women—United
States—Interviews. 3. Christians—United States—Interviews. I.
Title.
    BR526.L39 1989
208'.2—dc20

                                  89-32472
                                       CIP

89 90 91 92 93 94 95 96 97 98 - 10 9 8 7 6 5 4 3 2 1

For De

CONTENTS

CHAPTER ONE

Listening to Voices

On Father's Day, 1982, it dawned on me that my life was one great, grinding disappointment.

A typical Sunday, it began like many others. The traditional family unit (mom, dad, two small children) woke early, ate breakfast together, dressed up in best or cleanest clothes, drove to church and was distributed to various Sunday school classes: Ross to Door Slammers, Drake to the nursery, Steve and Alice to the Young Marrieds. For an hour, Ross toddled, Drake screamed, Steve pondered the paradoxes of God's purposes, and Alice pretended everything was peaches and cream.

Looking around our Sunday school class—forty other couples of similar age and circumstance—I assumed that their lives were perfectly in order and that I was the only one who was worried about money, disappointed in my children, unfulfilled in the role of stay-at-home mother, tired of being tired, and desperately wanting some positive change.

The sermon that day increased these feelings of isolation. Our minister spoke of his counseling with an infertile couple who had adopted a child. During their session they declared that parenthood was a nightmare: their child wasn't what they had in mind. These parents, my minister lamented, held their adoptive infant daughter at arm's length, referred to her as "it," and had come to him because they wanted to know how to go about returning the baby to the adoption agency.

If the scorn rippling through the congregation wasn't exactly audible, it was no less present.

"What kind of people are these?" asked the minister.

"What kind, indeed!" sniffed the congregation.

They are parents like me, I thought to myself. *That's the way I feel. The only difference is that I can't take my own flesh and blood back to anybody; I don't have the option of returning unwanted merchandise. I have to stick it out, even if it kills me.*

On Father's Day, 1982, I came home from church, locked myself in the bedroom and refused to come out. I wouldn't come out for a toddler banging on the door, for a baby who needed to nurse, or for a confused husband who just wanted to know if I was okay. *Okay?* No, I wasn't okay.

Because life—my life—wasn't turning out as I'd expected. All my assumptions were being challenged; my disappointment was overwhelming. My dreams were dying, one by one. And that being the case, I didn't see any reason why I should come out of the bedroom. At all. Ever.

THE AGE OF ENTITLEMENT

High-quality life is the goal of my generation. We're the baby boomers, the yuppies. We were born in the forties, fifties and sixties, raised in an era of optimism and hard work. We were told by our parents and teachers that we could be president of the United States, or at least chairman of General Motors. Our *Weekly Readers* promised that one day our cars would be replaced by helicopters; space travel would be routine; nuclear power would be safe and inexpensive; and our daily nutrition would come in the form of a single, tidy tablet. Imagine that! We were so special and so different from all previous generations that we wouldn't even have to eat food to stay alive.

As we grew into adolescence, we became a major force in the marketplace. Our allowances and the income we received from part-time jobs became the envy of manufacturers and retailers. Advertising cannons were leveled in our direction; department stores were refitted to appeal to our unique sense of style; fashions were designed for our adolescent bodies.

The blacks of my generation were promised freedom at last, and young women were told that they could do absolutely anything. No longer shackled by race or sex, we would make our way boldly into a world that had been closed to us for generations—the world of learning and prestige and wealth.

We scorned the politics and values of the generation which had sacrificed so much for us. We rejected the traditions and wisdom of our parents; we created our own rules. We intimidated our elders with our esoteric knowledge and with our sheer numbers. We believed in ourselves and in our ability to make our dreams come true.

We may have lost some of our idealism as we married and had children, as we made our way in the world, but the basic aspirations did not change. We still want the good life . . . whatever that is. To some it's a kitchen inhabited by Kitchenaids and Cuisinarts; to others, backpacking in Alaska. It may be a second computer for our brighter-than-average children or Jane Fonda's workout tapes on the VCR; organic tofu or unassailable tax shelters.

Pandering to our insecurities—am I really the quality person I can be, should be?—television shows, magazines, videos, and books tell us how to attain our goals for the good life: we are told how to make love, how to cook, how to enrich our children's early years, how to love ourselves, how to love our jobs, how to cocoon ourselves in our homes, how to buy art, how to sell our houses, how to prosper during the coming economic boom/depression, and how to avoid a mid-life crisis.

I am a Christian; surely that exempts me from this frantic striving, this ungodly pursuit of self. Yes? No. Not at all.

What it means is that *Redbook* sits on the coffee table next to the latest copy of a Christian women's magazine instructing me on how to raise children who love to sing Bible songs and how to be an effective member of the Outreach Committee at church. It means that the L.L. Bean catalog comes in the mail along with the Christian camping brochure. It means that after I peruse the self-help books at the local B. Dalton bookstore I can stroll down to the Christian Supply Center and be bombarded with titles instructing me in the practicalities of Biblical marriage, well-disciplined children, fitness ("for Jesus' sake"), home schooling, public schooling, spiritual direction, time management, dynamic housekeeping, counseling friends and relatives through troubled times. If I work hard enough, I can have it all—I can be the Proverbs 31 woman, that wife of noble character who brings food from afar, gets up in the middle of the night to cook it, plants vineyards, spins and weaves and sews, and runs a clothing outlet out of her garage—in her spare time, I suppose.

Is it any wonder then that I locked myself in the bedroom? As I look back on it, I can only be embarrassed—not surprised.

OPPORTUNITY KNOCKS

It is said that the flip side of every problem is an opportunity. If that's true, then opportunity virtually knocked down my suburban door on Father's Day, 1982. I did, at last, emerge from the bedroom later in the day to resume the normal duties of caring for home and children. But I had been brought to a place where I would seriously search for solutions to my problems and answers to my questions.

My main question was simplicity itself. Why is this so difficult? After all, bearing and raising children is the most natural thing in the world for a woman to do. My childhood was populated by women who had done their biological duty without depression or despair (so I thought)—why does it have me on the brink of disaster almost every minute of the day? What's wrong with me?

What was wrong seems obvious now, although at the time I didn't have a clue. For one thing, my body was in the middle of a postpartum depression. Not "baby blues," but a full-blown, hormonally activated and emotionally debilitating depression.

For another I was living 750 miles away from my nearest relative, in a part of the United States that, culturally, might just as well have been a foreign country to me. I was far from the support of my family and had few friends in the area.

Additionally, my expectations for life—expectations that had grown into my personality since I was a little girl—were unmet by my present experience.

It was just a matter of time before my hormones regained their equilibrium and I gradually emerged from my depression. It was great to have some emotional composure again! And then Steve and I decided to move back to Nebraska (state slogan: "Nebraska, The Good Life!") where we were raised and where our families still lived. We were embraced by family and by friends (some we had known since grade school days) and basked in the support and affection they offered us. Life did get better.

But my expectations didn't fade when the postpartum depression did, nor did they stay back in Memphis with our cat. And the subject of expectations and reality has occupied my thinking ever since . . . well, ever since Father's Day, 1982. This preoccupation with expectations has been an opportunity to do something about them—for my own sake and for the sake of others.

WRITE ON

When I wrote *The Christmas Book*, the subject of celebration was approached in this way: the Christmas season carries with it tremendous hopes—for financial prosperity, family togetherness, culinary accomplishment, spiritual renewal. Expectations are dangerously high. And the reality? In reality, children fight, in-laws frustrate, gift clothes don't fit, toys don't work, cookies get burned, and year after year we miss that true sense of epiphany we desire most.

My thesis went something like this: We must first identify our expectations and then reconcile the difference between those expectations and reality. We can do this by revising expectations or revising reality, or both.

This approach seemed helpful, and I began to think that my thesis might be applied successfully elsewhere. So in *The Lie of the Good Life*, the discussion of expectations and realities is being extended into a broader arena—the everyday lives of everyday women. In this book we will explore the expectations of family life, careers, health, spiritual development, accomplishment, and appearance.

But how can such a book be written? If I was to follow the tried-and-true formula (identify area of expressed interest, formulate approach to the issue, generate solutions relative to same), wouldn't that constitute yet another layer of expectations for the reader? Wouldn't that put just one more book on the shelf that promises perfection? Another easy, pre-packaged solution for difficult problems?

So many books are like that! Books by authors who write out of a single area of expertise, or who want to share a special story about a personal victory. A woman who excells in maintaining strong relationships writes a book about friendships. A retired missionary relates her experience of living in a foreign culture. The creative and innovative mother offers suggestions on how to plan memorable family activities. Writers mostly write from their expertise and success, of course.

But does Miss Congeniality discuss her crummy sex life? Never! Neither does the missionary mention the fact that none of her children have set foot in church since leaving home. The mother of those teenagers who are so ecstatic about family vacations in Historic Williamsburg may not have cooked a nutritious meal in twenty years.

Fair enough. But as long as we writers (and speakers) tout our successes and gloss over our failures, we perpetuate the myth that if one is committed in faith, vigilant in relationships, organized in habits, positive in outlook . . . the good life is well nigh inevitable.

What happens? The real woman who is living in the trenches begins to think that others succeed where she alone fails. She looks at the bookshelves and imagines a composite woman who can do it all, while she can do hardly anything. She may come to believe she is unique in her disappointments and failures. A suspicion of inadequacy creeps into her life, and with it comes isolation. Unable to articulate her frustrations, she becomes vaguely disconcerted and increasingly alone with her problems. She may even, I suppose, lock herself in the bedroom.

CONSULTING THE EXPERTS

Not wanting to increase further the distance between writers and readers, I decided to put this book in the hands of the true experts. Here's what I did: I interviewed fifty Christian women around the country. Some were friends, a few were family members; most were previously unknown to me, the result of networking based on personal recommendations. I traveled north, south, east, and west to get their stories. A few visited with me on the phone; some invited me to their homes; most were happy to meet in a restaurant over breakfast or lunch.

I usually began by explaining my purpose: to talk to ordinary women like myself, asking them to discuss their expectations for adult life, and to get their views and their wisdom on a variety of subjects that affect married women and mothers. (I chose to focus on wives and mothers because that's where my personal interest lies. Although not all the women I interviewed were married or had children, what they said is geared to those who are married or do have children.)

In the interest of protecting the privacy of those who contributed, each has been assigned a pseud-onym—some have been given more than one. In many cases it was important to change certain other details, such as their city of residence or the names of husbands and children. I wanted to make sure that each woman felt free to share honestly, especially since some of the contributors are well known in their own communities or even nationally.

Those who gave voice to their life stories are all women who claim faith in Christ. They are Protes-tants, Catholics, charismatics, fundamentalists, conser-vatives, moderates and liberals; practical women and mystical women; rich and poor; white women and women of color; northerners and southerners; farm women and city dwellers; midlanders and coast-dwellers. Their ages range from mid-twenties to mid-seventies.

SPEAKING FOR THE RECORD

Every interview followed its own path, depending on circumstances. And though the questions asked varied from person to person, most proceeded along these same lines:

• What kind of family did you grow up in?

• Did you have dreams of adult life when you were a little girl?

• Do you have any heroes? Any writers, speakers, public personalities that you ad-mire? Any characters from literature that have inspired or influenced you? Any mentors or gurus?

• What is your biggest frustration right now? What is your biggest joy?

• What were you looking for in marriage? In motherhood?

• Do you experience the romance you hoped for in your marriage? Do you want to talk about your sex life?

• How do you feel about the word *fulfillment*?

• What has been your major disappointment in life?

• Have you found serendipity in your life, joy you weren't expecting?

• What dreams did you have in the past?

• When you think of the future, how far ahead do you look, and what do you see?

A few women had difficulty understanding what I was getting at or why I wanted to talk to them about it ("I don't know if I really understand why you called me . . . What I have to say is pretty ordinary."). These were usually women who were not experiencing much difficulty reconciling life with their expectations. That doesn't mean they weren't important to talk to, or that you won't be reading what they had to say. On the contrary, it is very important to hear from women who don't have severely inflated expectations and who aren't living in perpetual anticipation of something better. I was inspired, sometimes even amazed, and always encouraged to talk to these women.

Most women I talked to, however, spoke of trashed dreams and the joy of serendipity. They identified the surprises and disappointments of life, times when reality is out of sync with expectations, in either a positive or negative way.

Typically, after a couple hours of interviewing, I was told: "Now, you've got to call my friend Hortense—she is such an achiever! I don't know how she keeps it all together. Talk about a person who has a lot of expectations in her life . . . well, Hortense would be perfect for this."

So I would call Hortense and say that I'd been talking to Matilda, and Matilda was enthusiastic about Hortense and . . . This is the way the networking went; this is the way I was able to interview fifty women starting with just a handful of friends and acquaintances (and I could easily have found a hundred more).

OPENING UP A DIALOGUE

I was asking women to share their lives, and as they did, I could not remain detached. I wasn't Ted Koppel interviewing the president's Chief of Staff. I was a woman, a mother, a wife, a Christian talking to another woman who shared many of my concerns, if not my opinions.

There were times I had to bite my tongue—several women had definite views about women who worked outside the home (they were against it), and here I was, taking it all down while my husband and children were fending for themselves at home, two thousand miles away. Yet I appreciated their candor and wouldn't have wanted them to hold back their opinions just because I was the embodiment of their criticism!

At times, it was difficult to keep my amazement tactful. "You're kidding!" I wanted to gasp. "You mean you haven't had sex for two years?" Or maybe it was, "Every night? Really? Wow!"

There were times when I was fairly bursting with advice, and it was hard work keeping quiet; sometimes I couldn't help myself and spoke up, offering jewels from my vast treasure trove of wisdom.

And while there were times when we had to stop the interview for tears—theirs and mine—there were as many times when we had to turn off the tape until we quit laughing and could get back on the subject.

I would leave an interview feeling baffled, or encouraged, or challenged, or sometimes just feeling safe. On several occasions I went away thanking God for the easy life I lead.

VOICES ON PAPER

It's one thing to listen to someone talk about her life; it's another entirely to get those words down on paper (not to mention into a book) so that they're understood by a reader in the way the speaker intended—a much more difficult task than it might first appear.

When the interviews were finished, I was left with boxes full of cassette tapes. These, in time, became boxes full of typed transcriptions of those tapes. And then? Many women who seemed wonderfully articulate when I was interviewing them turned out to be well nigh incomprehensible when their words hit paper. As I pored over their tapes and transcriptions, I realized that their eyes, facial expressions, and gestures had comprised the greatest part of their communication; their body language spoke volumes. But those visual cues are not available to a reader; I had to help these women be understood.

There was also a good deal of routine editing: redundancies have been cut and lengthy passages pruned, along with language that might prove offensive to some readers. This is tampering with reality, of course, because in real life we do tend to repeat ourselves and go on and on about certain subjects. Even though the length has been trimmed, and the expletives deleted, the blood and guts of the stories remain.

LISTENING TO VOICES

This book is not a bowl of popcorn—something to be devoured in one sitting. This is rich material. Take it too fast and you'll miss most of what it has to offer. Try to absorb too much and you could become very frustrated and confused. I suggest that you read at your leisure, little bits at a sitting. Feel free to dip in and out. This is not a novel; you can skip chapters and come back to them later. This book is made for dabbling.

I hope and believe these voices will speak for themselves, and that the truth of God can be gleaned from them—and that this can happen without the benefit of any expert's interpretation. I will try to provide throughout the book opportunities and encouragements for you to think through what is being said—for in the end, you must draw your own conclusions.

That's because there's more wisdom on these pages than I know, since it's the wisdom of dozens of women who have experienced, understood, and intuited more about life than I have—or possibly ever will. If I summarize too much, judge too much, evaluate too much, if I wrap it all up in a nice, neat package . . . well, the package will only be as big as I am. And that's not big enough.

Life's truths are rarely laid out for us 1-2-3, a-b-c. We struggle to make sense of our circumstances and situations. For that reason you will encounter no completed stories. There are no obituaries on these pages. Each woman who speaks is *alive*. Whether she is twenty-five, forty-five, or seventy-five, she is in the midst of the struggles, joys, difficulties, and blessings of life. Many of the contributors have, to my certain knowledge, experienced important changes of circumstances and changes of heart since I interviewed them. Nothing here is static.

Life goes on. Nobody who is truly alive is looking back at a finished story. At best, some are able to see that certain chapters of their lives have come to a close, and can offer the wisdom of perspective. But please don't expect to hear concise summaries or benedictions. Rather, expect to encounter shortsightedness, the confusion of the moment, disorganization, and ambiguity.

I am convinced that it is important to hear these voices. It is important to step out of the safety zone we maintain around us, important to open ourselves emotionally and spiritually to the women who speak through these pages just as they have opened themselves to us.

It is an issue of trust. Each of these women claims Christ's presence and authority in her life. Faith is the common ground, the tie that binds us all together here. It would be unseemly to discount what one or another reveals simply because her experience is not our own or a specific belief doesn't mesh with ours.

You may be tempted to say that one of these women is less committed, less in God's will, less in relationship with him because the thoughts, beliefs and doubts she expresses don't fit into your notion of how a Christian woman should act or think. You may be tempted to say, "Well she's obviously not much of a Christian!" Please, don't. It is a trap, for in doing so you will have subjected a real person's real life to a casual judgment and reinforced your own prejudices. You will squander an opportunity to learn and grow.

We are inextricably bound up in the lives of these women. They are our sisters, neighbors, and friends. We sit beside them in church each Sunday. They live next door; we greet them when we take our children to school. They are integral parts of the body of Christ of which we are all members. Look for yourself in this book; look for your friends.

Now to each reader I extend an invitation: participate in the discussion already begun with these women of faith; listen to the wisdom contained in their experiences and insights; struggle with the complexities of life; seek personal growth as you hear the voices.

CHAPTER TWO

We've Got High Hopes

"The child is father of the man," and childhood seems the logical place to look for the earliest and most profound influences on adult life. Sabine, Barbara and Virginia—all women in their fifties—remember clearly the childhood experiences that have shaped their current expectations:

> **Sabine:** As a child, I never questioned that I could do and be whatever I wanted. The message was, "You can do anything." And the second part was the hard bit for me. "And you'd better!" It was expected that I would be as wonderful as my sister and brother.

> **Barbara:** My early childhood was harsh. We were living in China as missionaries, during the Japanese-Communist invasion. There was a lot of running, a lot of hiding, a lot of danger. I witnessed murder and torture. I lived on a raft in the middle of the Yellow River for three weeks. My brother and sister were put in a prison camp and stayed there for five years; we finally had to leave China without them. This called for a great deal of independence. I can understand how my

mother developed that strong, uncommunicative personality. It was necessary.

When we came to the United States, we moved to a tiny town in Michigan that seemed filled with ordinariness. There was no opportunity to see people operating at different levels, to see people who were successful. If people had "made it," they left. It was a boring little town. Most of the people seemed to come from a low- to middle-class background. Nobody was very rich or very poor.

That was very influential in my developing belief that life's tasks are pretty simple, and you shouldn't expect too much. Because I felt I was not very bright, not very gifted, not very capable, I tended to accept this view of life.

Therefore, my long-range expectations, or goals, were pretty modest, pretty small. I started with *such* low expectations of life giving me anything . . . I really expected nothing. So I've had few disappointments. It took a long time to accept that I was not really limited by lack of ability.

> **Virginia:** When I was growing up, it was this:
> Good, better, best;
> Never let it rest
> Until your good is better
> And your better best.

LITTLE MISS PERFECT

Nedra was one of many who talked of growing up in a family environment where perfection was the norm and anything less was unacceptable:

> The expectation that my parents had for my brothers and me was, certainly, that we would be . . . perfect. We'd get good grades, we'd excel in

the arts, we'd behave with poise and decorum, we'd be obedient children and devout Christians.

My parents expected me to be perfect; not only that, they expected me to believe that *they* were perfect. And that our family was perfect. In fact, they would even talk about how our family was perfect, how we had such a good family life. And I believed for a long time that we were all perfect.

When I left home, though, I realized that they weren't perfect, and the natural next step was to realize that I wasn't perfect, either.

I remember once trying to explain to my mother that things weren't okay with me. But she wouldn't hear of it. She said, "You've got a loving husband, a healthy child, a nice house, financial security; you can't be unhappy."

She just wasn't willing to entertain the idea that even with all that, I might be restless or dissatisfied or have some things that were lacking in my life. It wasn't okay to be "wanting" under those circumstances. It wasn't okay to be lonely.

I feel victimized by perfectionism. The expectations have been so strong that they constituted a complete ignoring of my needs. *I* wasn't important anymore. I was just a way of fulfilling their high expectations of perfection.

Bette: In my family, if you got a C, then it should have been a B and if you brought home a B, why wasn't it an A? So I was raised with this idea that you should always be striving.

I was taught I could never hit the mark, no matter how hard I tried, so I began to think I was of little value. That kind of programming is very deeply ingrained.

It also made me critical of others—including my husband. If James brought me a rose, I wanted it to be three; if he brought a half-dozen, I wanted a full dozen. I was never satisfied with what he did; I was always wanting him to do something more. I could not savor the one rose, enjoy it, appreciate it as an expression of his love and care for me.

It's only by remembering my position before the Lord that I can regain my sense of value. I'm not a person of value because of what I do or what I don't do. I'm valuable because of the Lord. And so is James. It's not to say that there aren't struggles; I still tend to want James to do something different from what he's doing. But I have a better base to work from.

Meredith: My parents were very, very poor. They grew up in a mill town in poverty. But my grandmother didn't do her own laundry. Never! She wouldn't have considered it. She sent her laundry out to be done—by an even poorer black woman I suppose. Of course, a shirt wasn't washed after each wearing.

My grandmother kept her home so clean you could eat off the floors—I've heard my father say that dozens of times. But she didn't have to do what I have to do. I know that my house isn't very neat.

Almost all my expectations for marriage came from my family—my parents, my aunts and uncles, and my older sisters.

Once we grow up and leave our family of birth to start our own families, we begin to see at a distance what was unclear close-up. When she left home, Nedra realized her family wasn't perfect, and Bette sees that the moving target of perfectionism she chased during her childhood caused her to be critical and unaccepting of others. Happily, such reflection has helped her understand that her ultimate value is not dependent on what she does, but who she is. Unhappily, many of the women I talked to are still obsessed with perfectionism.

DADS, HUSBANDS, AND FATHERS

If young men want to marry a girl just like the girl who married dear old dad, young women are influenced in their choice of a husband—and what they come to expect from that husband—by their fathers. Contrary to the song lyric, however, not many of the women I talked to wanted to marry someone like their fathers; most saw the flaws in their male parent and resolved to find someone different.

> **Juliet:** My parents' marriage was very traditional. My mother did all the work around the house, including the yard work. My dad worked at his job, brought home his paycheck, and sat in front of television.
>
> My mother always stressed that I should get a job so that I wouldn't be stuck in the house like her.

> **Wendy:** I had a very strong mother who kind of pushed my dad around. Their method of communication was for her to pick, and for him to clam up. My goal was that we would not communicate like that in our marriage.

> **Tricia:** I grew up on a farm, and the differences between men and women were very well defined. The men and boys took care of the machinery and the animals; as a girl, I was definitely in the house with Mom.

My mother had a job, once, when I was in high school. But it caused immediate marital problems, so she quit. She never again worked outside the home until my father died.

For my father, parenting was largely a matter of yelling, "Eunice, take care of those children of yours!" and coming around with the belt when it was needed. That's just the way he was.

Once my mother had to go away for five days. During that time my dad didn't do anything around the house. The dishes just sat there. I was expected to take care of it; I was a twelve-year-old, and I was the only girl in the family. It was my responsibility.

Perry is much more open about his emotions than my father was. I think he comes from a family that is healthier than mine in this sense. He's much more involved with our kids, much more sensitive and loving. Maybe my dad was caring, but he didn't show it. Perry shows it.

Suzanne: My father is bisexual. And he molests little boys. I didn't know this until I was twenty-six. My mother told me; she wanted to know if my father's behavior had anything to do with my brother's mental illness. She wanted to know if I thought he had ever molested my brother. I told her I didn't think so.

But I *do* think he molested my brother. My brother hates my father, of course, and so do I. And he didn't molest me.

I really hoped I would marry a man who would take care of me. I had such a longing for it, and I suppose it's because my father, who is also an alcoholic, never did take care of me.

When I married Garth, he was going to finish college, then we'd move to Utah where he'd study architecture, and when he was done with school, we'd have three children. Just like that. Settled. None of it happened.

I can see now that it was an unrealistic expectation—and maybe an unhealthy one, too, this business of having a man take care of me.

JEANINE AND ROGER: THE EARLY YEARS

Women often enter marriage with expectations that arise from their birth family. Whether they want to duplicate a happy home or avoid a second-generation disaster, they're viewing the family in which they grew up as the point of departure, and the family they create with their husband will be either better or worse than that.

Inevitably, differences in family background will cause friction. **Jeanine** was eloquent about the adjustment frustrations she and her husband experienced during the first year of their marriage.

I grew up in a moral home, a church-going home. It was not a Christian home. My mother cooked, did Girl Scouts and 4-H, and made our Halloween costumes. My father was supportive, but pursued his life on a parallel track. He watched a lot of TV, a typical American father of the fifties.

I vowed that my marriage wouldn't be like that. It wouldn't be segmented, with me in my world and my husband in his. My mother says that I looked for someone who didn't want a TV and wasn't a sports enthusiast. I don't think it was that concrete.

Roger and I shared a common interest in the mechanics of marriage. We dated in the early seventies. Then, every little thing was discussed and picked apart. "What would you feel if you knew that I felt such-and-such . . . ?"

Even with all this communication, I cried through the first year of marriage.

Do you know why?*

Unmet expectations about little things. We came up with a phrase that we would use to identify the source of this conflict: "You're criticizing my background."

Sometimes we've been able to compromise, but there are some things that I've just had to give up. For example, our wedding was traditional in that it was given and paid for by my parents . . . who planned to have champagne and wedding toasts . . . which was totally unacceptable to Roger's family. The day before the ceremony, we were talking about plans, and I said, "So-and-so will do the first toast," and his sister said, "What toast?" with the color draining from her face. And although the champagne was bought, I let my parents know that there could be no drinking because Roger's family was so opposed to it.

They said, "What do you mean? How can you have a wedding without drinking?" But I took Roger's family's side of the issue and was more willing to have my parents and their friends offended than to offend his family. So I guess I made the decision pretty early in our relationship that his family's way of doing things was automatically more "Christian" than my family's way—because his family was, indeed, Christian, and mine wasn't.

*Editor's note: Boldface type indicates the author's questions or comments.

It hasn't been such big issues of life for us, but things like should you have stockings at Christmas, should we carve the turkey slices thin or thick, who should barbecue?

Man's work, if you ask me.

That's what I thought. I thought he should be able to cook food on the grill. It was eight years after Roger and I were married that my mother told me that when there was barbecuing to be done, she looked up in the cookbook how many minutes on each side and handed the meat to my dad with specific instructions on what to do. I didn't know this. I perceived that my father innately knew how to be an outdoor chef. I thought that the mother handed the meat to the father and that he brought it back done to perfection. I wondered why my husband couldn't or wouldn't do this simple thing.

It was our background. Roger's father couldn't boil water, and to expect Roger to be a fabulous outdoor chef like my father—who apparently wasn't one, anyway—was ridiculous.

A lot of our disagreements came around the holidays. Christmas was a ritual in my family; you did the same things year after year. And these things were important and made special. Like the Christmas tree. My parents still have a tree like the Nutcracker. And his parents have some weed from the backyard! So how do we reconcile this in our own family? Roger says it's not as Christian to spend a lot of money on a pagan symbol. I think that picking out the tree should be a family event, something really important.

We've each bent some in resolving these issues.

You Be Desi, I'll Be Lucy

Those of us who grew up watching television can't help having been influenced by it. Young girls who watched "I Love Lucy," "Lassie," "Ozzie and Harriet," or "Leave It to Beaver" were presented with a picture of a beautiful housewife with a hair-sprayed pageboy who wore full skirts, heels and pearls around the house; who served a hot breakfast to her family every morning; who was married to a man who worked in "the office"; who lived in a town with a happy-sounding name like "Springfield" or "Centerville." Children in these TV families sometimes got into mischief, but before the half-hour was over they had—thanks to the loving guidance of their parents—seen the error of their ways and come out on the other side wiser and more adorable than ever.

Lucy Ricardo, Laura Petrie, and Harriet Nelson may have had career aspirations, but their families always came first. There was never any question of arranging day-care so they could finish a college degree or re-enter the marketplace. Their husbands had steady work, they had nice clothes and comfortable homes in those golden pre-VISA and MASTERCARD days. Life was grand.

I grew up on a steady diet of this view of life and motherhood. So great was the power of the media and my personal admiration for Mary Tyler Moore and June Lockhart that I never consciously tested the television images against the real life I could observe in my own home or neighborhood.

Consequently, it came as a bit of a shock when I realized that my post-partum stomach wasn't going to lie flat like Lucille Ball's did after she had given birth to Little Ricky, or that I couldn't trust my children to drink out of those nice crystal glasses that June Cleaver let Beaver and Wally pour their milk into. Or that Steve wouldn't solve all our domestic problems because, after all, "Father Knows Best."

A friend of mine is trying her best to recapture the glory of those simpler, less complicated times. She now gets "Leave It to Beaver" on cable and wrote me recently that she's been making it a point to dress up in pearls, ruffled apron and heels just like June. "That's all," she wrote, "nothing else. Just pearls, ruffled apron, and heels!"

> **Linda:** I had an ideal in mind, I think partly because of "Leave It to Beaver" and "Ozzie and Harriet." But my expectations from all my reading and exposure to TV were so far apart from my reality that I didn't know how to carry out my dream because I didn't have that modeling in my own family.
>
> Then I turned to the counterculture to enter another dream world because, in a way, that was just as unreal. I think the counterculture offered women as much real fulfillment as "Make Room for Daddy" did—not much!

> **Sabine:** My father died when I was thirteen, and I felt his absence as a man terribly. I would fantasize all day that Rock Hudson—or some man—would come into my life and take care of me. Save me. I felt that my father, who had always looked after me, had to be replaced, and it was up to me to find the man who would be my father for me.
>
> If my father had lived, I'm sure I would have had those adolescent fantasies anyway. But I probably wouldn't have lived them out so completely. I probably wouldn't have gotten married when I was twenty—to a strong, handsome man

who I thought would make me worthwhile and take care of me.

Patricia: My cultural influences come out of the romanticism of the forties. Walt Disney's *Snow White, Cinderella.* I remember getting a bride doll for Christmas when I was five. That was the dream of my parents' generation and it was passed on to me—getting a white dress and marrying a handsome man. After World War II there was a romanticism about the family.

I used to love to watch "I Love Lucy." To this day, I kind of expect George to laugh at me when I mess up, like Desi laughed at Lucy.

Juliet: When I was in high school and college, I was preoccupied with the idea that I wanted to get married. At that time I read a lot of romance fiction, and I tried to conform myself to media images of what an attractive (to me) woman was. I thought that these things would help my chances of getting married, I suppose.

But as I grew out of adolescence and then got married, I quit worrying about these things. I don't really think about the *Playboy* centerfold or the TV housewife anymore. When I was younger, I did; but I didn't have much self-confidence then. Now I do. I've done some things and done them well. I know who I am, and I don't have to look to these things to define myself.

Would that we could all put our expectations behind us with that kind of maturity. How did Juliet do it? How did she see the light? Perhaps it was a simple maturing. Yet I've matured but still I'm struggling. Jane Pauley is one year older than I am, and watching the "Today" show always reminds me that she's more successful, thinner and smarter than I am. The show offers me a daily reminder of her achievements and my failures. I'm inferior to thousands of women, and that's a fact, but her superiority is something I'm confronted with five days a week—and that's a drag.

WE READ ALL ABOUT IT

The print media are having an impact on our expectations, too. So I asked women to tell me what kinds of magazines they read, and how they feel about recent books.

Sue Ellen: Most of the women's magazines that are out now are self-centered. They have articles about how you can make everything work out better for *you*. I don't think that's good for me to read. Same with a lot of fiction. If it's a book about a woman having an affair . . . why should I be reading that? It doesn't do me any good.

I do read *some*. I don't like to have these magazines sitting around the house because my daughter picks them up, and I think that she could get the wrong idea. And I won't let myself have a steady diet of Donahue and Oprah Winfrey. On the other hand, I like to make a conscious effort to keep up with what's going on, and with how other people think. So I read some, not much.

Emily: My aunt gives me a Christian women's magazine as a Christmas gift every year.

Do you read it?

Only for laughs. I write it all off—I'm really terrible. It does not relate to me at all. It's all the same stories. Like: "How the Lord has opened my eyes." Like: "How I was a burned-out mother of four, and my friend Marge called one day and said, 'You need to meet the Lord' and that was exactly what I needed and we had a cup of tea and now I have the Lord in my life and my life is perfect." Like that.

It's too pat. Too "gospely."

Well, maybe I'll write an article for it someday. I'll get burned out and my friend will drink tea with me and I'll see the light. So I'll eat my words. But for now, I just can't get anything out of it.

If I get time to read these days I'll read Raymond Chandler or P.G. Wodehouse. What do I need with *American Baby*? I'm with a baby all day. The last thing I need is to read about diaper rash or how to get her to eat her cereal.

Redbook? I don't have time to try out new recipes. I don't need to look at *Cosmopolitan* and see all those beautiful bodies. I don't care about the five new shades of lipstick for spring.

Ingrid: I can read *Good Housekeeping* and have no problems, but if I pick up magazines and books that are telling Christian women how to be everything they can be—it makes me sick. Really. I mean how to write individualized devotions for your kids and all that kind of stuff! If I read that and take it to heart, I'll feel like a failure. I'll just focus on everything I could do that I'm not doing.

Am I a failure? No. I can look at my children, look at my marriage, and see that it's going okay. Not easy, but okay. I am not a failure, but there's nobody here to tell me that. There are, though, a lot of people here to tell me what else I should be doing, or what I should be doing differently or better. They're writing articles and even whole books about that.

I can't afford to listen to them. If I did I'd probably commit hara-kari. I can't live on an up-and-down, up-and-down roller coaster. Life is too short. I don't need the stress; I don't want the stress; I don't think that God intends for me to take on the stress.

Another thing: I find Christian women's magazines and books condescending. They talk down to me; they assume that I'm not interested in world affairs, theology, big issues. They think all I'm interested in is summer activities for children and recipes for potluck suppers. I don't read books about how to get organized, how to entertain. I haven't found any that have challenged me as a Christian, as a person. They only want to talk to me about women-things.

I'm a Christian first; I'm a woman second. There's very little challenge for me as a Christian in most women's books. So I end up reading the "boy stuff."

Marilyn: Lots of times I agree with whatever I'm reading at the moment, until I have a chance to think about it further and realize that it disagrees with something I believe.

You're susceptible?

I'm idealistic, and sometimes I have to fight my idealism. It doesn't always serve me well. I find it easy to get a wonderful vision of the way things *ought* to be.

It's enlightening to read old books on marriage and family—books from the fifties, usually written by men, on what a good wife is and does. It's usually very offensive by today's standards. However, if you put the advice of these books into the social ecology of the time that they were written, maybe they aren't so bad. Maybe they were good advice for those times. There certainly is a mood in these older books that women are *not* a force to be reckoned with. There isn't a lot of respect for women's abilities.

Denise: I feel a lot of pressure to look good, to look a certain way. It seems that I'm always worried about my hair not being right—being stringy or straight. Having fat thighs—I'm always worried about that.

When I look at women's magazines, I get obsessed with looking good. Boy, I feel like I should have matured beyond the point where my looks matter so much, but for some reason I haven't. I try to avoid women's magazines, and I avoid going shopping. There's a huge pressure on women who work to have the right look for their job. To dress for success. I hate this pressure, but I know that I'm very vulnerable to it.

I'd like to be like Hope in "thirtysomething." They show her in her underwear, and it's like she's got no thighs. She's attractive, appealing in a very natural way. Her husband is crazy about her, and her husband is gorgeous. She's smart, she has a healthy baby. She struggles with her problems, but she's equal to the task.

Here I am wanting my life to be like a television show! How stupid!

PURE ILLUSION

Many of us are harboring illusions of life that are virtually irreconcilable with reality.

The most common illusion I encountered was the "knight-in-shining-armor" fantasy. One woman confessed, "I was under the impression that I was waiting for the perfect man." Another called her marriage expectation "typical": that her husband would make her happy.

Janet: My early assumptions about marriage were like Cinderella. I thought I'd marry this wonderful guy, and we'd live happily ever after. In *The Cinderella Syndrome*, Lee Ezell says to remember that when you marry your knight in shining armor, you have to clean up after his horse.

I suppose a lot of women go into marriage as I did, thinking that our marriages will be special. Maybe not a fairy tale—but at least not as bad as they've turned out to be. We find that our dreams are shattered, as we realize that we can't change the men we've married.

Sue Ellen: I thought I'd get married, I'd work a few years, and then we'd have babies and I'd stay home and play with the babies. I never gave a thought to the fact that those babies would turn into teenagers. I didn't think to marry somebody who could deal well with teenagers.

Aggie: I had this dream: to work and do research. Then I changed that dream to another one: to get married and have children. Of course, we wouldn't have arguments like other married couples. We talked about this quite a bit before we got married: how we would have a Christian marriage, and we wouldn't have fights.

Marsha: In my doctor's office there is a picture of three women. One is reclining on a chaise lounge, holding an eighteen-month-old child, giving him a bottle; another is standing behind her in the classic Madonna pose, with her hand resting on the top of her protruding, pregnant tummy; the third is sitting in a chair nursing her baby. It's all lace and velvet and ribbons and curls

41

and soft focus and pastels. The caption on this picture is "Reflections on Motherhood."

When I first became pregnant and started going to the doctor for examinations, I would look at that picture and think it was pretty nice. But as my pregnancy progressed, and then after Stephanie was born, I came to see how ridiculous and misleading that picture is.

There are some who would like to idolize motherhood; children are the ultimate toy. We can dress them in cute clothes, and we can coach them on what to say and do. But the problem with that is that children and mothers, by their very nature, strive against those simpering images and false appearances. Mothering is not soft-edged and fuzzy. It's often sharp and dirty and earthy and muddy and smelly and rough. The Dreft mother—with her white dress and perfumed soap—is misleading. Life isn't like that. Not my life, anyway.

Irene: I had expected that there would be a sense of completeness or security—that the hard work would be done—at my age. [Irene is in her fifties.] I kept thinking that if I could just get through with raising my children or finishing my education or building my business . . . that it would be "over." It took me a fairly long time to realize that won't be the case. There's always one more thing that leaves me with an open end in my life.

It isn't that these things I've done haven't been satisfying, but they haven't been enough.

WHAT'S WORTH KEEPING?

Even as I share with you the thoughts and recollections of these women, I begin to feel overwhelmed by the many expectations that come at us from every direction. And questions spring to mind. Is there such a thing as a positive, inspiring expectation? Why are some people battered by expectations while others are encouraged by them? Is it good to have expectations, or is it bad?

In order to grow personally I have to ask myself: where do my expectations come from? Is it right that I have taken them on? Are there some that I should have shrugged off? Are there others I should have assimilated? Where are my expectations leading me? As a Christian, I wonder what God's expectations are for me, and where they fit in with all those television shows I've watched, with what I observed in my own home, what I was taught by my peers and teachers, what I have drawn from my culture and times.

I can see that some expectations are silly, some are hurtful, some are unrealistic. But I know that I can't live without expectations. To do so would be to have no guiding purpose, no standard against which to measure growth, no mission in life.

> **Janet:** I think that expectations of yourself, expectations of your spouse, what you perceive God to expect of you . . . these have a tremendous effect on your life. I know that my own expectations for myself are the most unrealistic of any of these. God just has to get me to a place where he can talk to me about these things.

That's it exactly! That's why I'm so interested in all of this. I'm exactly that way. A friend who contributed to this book is judging expectations this way: "You have to figure it out: Is this something that someone else has for me that I'm trying to live up to, or is it really from the Lord? If it is, what comes from the Lord is gentle, it's kind and pure, it's easily entreated, it's a different feeling from a taskmaster who sits over me and says you must do this, and you must do this."

Whatever the source of our expectations—events of childhood, input from parents, media, society—we should eventually ask ourselves what God expects. His expectations are worth fulfilling.

Have you felt a kinship—a sisterly feeling—with any of the women in this chapter? Did anyone recount an experience you too have experienced?

It's not too difficult to feel connected with those who share our background or opinions. But what about those who have had different experiences and outlooks? We can expand our world by trying to at least respect their opinions; eventually we may come to understand and empathize, even if we never fully agree.

My college drama coach insisted that all good actors like people. This general feeling of affection for the human race makes it possible for them to create convincing characterizations. A good actor, he said, believes this: most people are doing the best they can under the circumstances. If that is our belief, we can forgive a lot; we can accept a lot.

Having made some progress in identifying the source of our expectations—finding out where they come from—then it's logical that we proceed from that to a more detailed examination of the impact these expectations are having on our lives, and how we're coping in the important arenas.

On we go, then, listening to more voices.

COLLEEN'S STORY

As she nears her fortieth birthday, Colleen is finding growth in the disappointments, failures, and inevitable crises of life, she's coming to accept her own limitations and God's sovereignty.

As I think about expectations, I believe that the first time I ever got thrown was when my mom died. The second time was when I got a divorce. I simply could not accept the fact that what I wanted and worked for wouldn't come true. I didn't get my way about something that was vitally important to me.

GETTING RID OF PAIN

I think we're born with some spiritual understanding and drivenness about finding love, but I experienced love fully when I became a Christian in high school.

My father was an alcoholic; the family environment I grew up in was tenuous and insecure. My goal was to get rid of the pain in my life. I didn't have an early image of what my future would be like, but I was driven in an intense way to get rid of that pain: the feeling of being not quite complete, not quite right.

I thought, *Well, I need to find a man who will fix me, who will make me complete, who will help me see myself as a whole being.*

My first and most basic criteria for choosing a mate was that he, too, would be a fundamentalist Christian. I believed that our marriage would last forever, because it's *supposed* to last forever if you do it right, and didn't I do it right? I really thought there was a path in life—the straight and narrow. And if you're on the straight and narrow, things are good. I *knew* I was doing everything in my power to stay on the straight and narrow, and I was convinced that I would be protected from bad things. God would see to it that I was safe. He'd reward me for being good.

Marrying Mike seemed like the right thing to do at the time, and I was doing it the best I knew how. But the marriage was not a place where I could escape this pain, this pain that I'd felt since I was a little child. I went into it thinking Mike was supposed to make me happy. He was the kind of person who took responsibility, and that was supposed to do the trick. But he couldn't— he couldn't *make* me happy. He tried, but he got worn out.

I had a tape playing that said I could do better in my marriage than my mother did. Of course, my parents *should* have gotten a divorce; they had no business being together. But I didn't see that divorce was an option for me. I clung to the belief that even if there was unbearable pain, there were other ways of coping.

"Well, heck," said I, "I can figure out what's wrong in a given situation; and I'm tenacious enough to change whatever it is that's wrong so that it will be right. I'll work my magic! I'll fix anything! I'll be good, I'll work hard, I'll change the facts!" So I felt like a failure; I didn't do what I said I was going to do: make a good marriage.

I've broken a lot of rules I have by getting a divorce. Like: YOU ALWAYS DO WHAT'S BEST FOR YOUR KIDS, REGARDLESS. In reality, maybe it's better for them that Mike and I are divorced. But maybe not, too. And I broke the rule that says: LIFE WILL BE GOOD IF YOU DO IT RIGHT.

When I was a little girl, my dad was the cause of my pain. When I was married, I thought Mike was the cause of my pain. Now I realize that I have to take the responsibility myself. I have to learn to deal with it.

I don't feel victimized by this divorce. If I did, maybe it would be easier to take. But I feel very, very responsible for what happened. I feel at fault, I feel guilty.

Divorce hasn't been a good thing, but I've learned a lot; and, for me, a lot of good has come out of it. Still, I'm relentless enough to say that it may not have been the only way we could settle our differences. And I'm hopeful enough to say, Okay, we've both grown up now. We're better people. Let's get back together.

The other day a friend told me, "Why, you're June Cleaver! That's what's going on in your life. You just need to get another Ward!"

That's true, probably. I have a heavy burden to create a perfect family to make up for the imperfect family of my childhood.

It's very hard for me to change my expectations, because it's very hard for me to accept defeat. But I have been defeated in some bottom-line, core areas of my life. My dreams have been shattered. Changing has been hard.

UNDERSTANDING GOD

Until my mom died, I had never prayed for anything I hadn't gotten. I couldn't *believe* that she wasn't being healed! When God had answered my prayers about so many little things, why wouldn't he answer my prayers about a very big, important thing?

When she died, I had a pretty young faith. And I can see that the other Christians around me supported my immaturity: the kind of naiveness that has answers for everything, that has God all figured out. You see, I used to pray for parking places—and get them! I would pray for someone in my sorority, and inside of a month she would have become a Christian. I had it all figured out. My mom's death changed everything.

Somehow, I came into life with an expectation that if I worked hard enough, I could do anything. I had an invincibleness that wouldn't die. But, I was being beaten by the fact that my mom was dying.

Now I can say that I'm understanding God a little bit better. And I am certainly understanding myself better. I still have these delusions of grandeur—like I can do anything—and at the same time I can feel incredibly incompetent. On the whole, I've grown up.

In what way?

I understand it. I get "it." I spent a couple years being mad at God, because I was sure that he had something to do with it. That was immaturity, a lack of understanding about free will.

How did you get it?

An intense study of life, and God. Prayer. Time. It was a maturing, spiritually.

I've spent the past thirty years figuring out the meaning of life. Is it A or is it B? The answer is, Both. It's A and it's B, too. This isn't cynicism, or a compromise cop-out. It means that life is rich, and God is ineffable, and everything isn't black-and-white.

I think that this is human consciousness—the ability to hold two competing truths in your life simultaneously and to know that even though they contradict themselves, they are both true.

Like the sayings: "Look before you leap," and "He who hesitates is lost." They are both true. Or "I participate in the divine as a child of God," and "I am a flop, a failure, a disappointment, a dry bit of dirt."

This is where I part company with the fundamentalists, you see, those fundamentalists who can find an answer for every problem and a judgment of every situation in the Bible. I don't believe that this approach is mature; I don't think it is the sort of approach that recognizes human consciousness or, for that matter, the sovereignty and greatness of God.

I have no problem with a simplistic approach to God as long as it is the *approach* and not the ultimate awareness reached. I see it as a way to faith, a place to start; but for growing Christians, I think that inevitably they will come to the point where a simple, cut-and-dried, I've-got-the-answer, here-look-it-up-in-the-Bible faith is left behind for one that has you standing in awe of the majesty of God, open to his truth, and less certain of all the *answers* but more certain of God.

It's a movement from the concrete to the abstract which is, I believe, a higher mode of thinking. God is, of course, concrete—that's what the incarnation is all about. But he's also abstract. We've got to keep that in mind as we pore over the Bible for his word about whether or not women should stay at home with their children, and if priests should marry, and if it's wrong to drive a Cadillac, or if Christians should run for public office. Abstract thinking has to be applied to these modern concrete situations.

You think you should grow up at twenty-one or twenty-three. Now I feel blessed to have done it at thirty-six! Actually, I thought I was growing up in my twenties. Getting married, getting a job, having children. This seemed like growth. But to survive my mother's death and my divorce—that really *has* been growth.

CHAPTER THREE

Tradition and Innovation

*N*early every woman I talked with responded in some way to the issue of "traditional womanhood." Granted, they had different ideas of what that entailed. To the older women, "traditional" meant lifelong devotion to husband and family. Middle-aged women tended to think in similar terms—although, having been touched by the women's movement after most of them had made marriage and family decisions, some were baffled by the existence of alternatives later in life where none had previously existed. Among the younger women, I noted two distinct trends: roughly half took it as a given that since they possessed certain job skills, they were entitled to practice those skills, family or no. The other half were committed to the family ethic of the older women, insisting that a woman's place is caring for husband and family, especially while children are still living at home.

GRAPPLING WITH CHOICES

Even those women who had grown up in an environment that strongly urged them to assume traditional roles were eventually confronted with alternatives. Generations ago, children followed in the footsteps of their parents without question. But the word *choice* kept cropping up in the interviews. The women's movement was repeatedly—and rightly!—associated with the proliferation of choices . . . and expectations.

Marilyn spoke for many when she talked about the shifts in her thinking over the past twenty years:

> I did listen to the women in the early seventies who were saying that a women's place is in the House . . . and in the Senate. On one hand, I had a conviction that I should be home with my children, but on the other hand I was open to the idea that I should be out there slaying dragons. I *did* stay home with the kids, but I *felt* that I might be doing something different.
>
> I actually became very defensive about it—I wrote articles about how women should be at home. I professionalized my conviction that I didn't need an outside profession. And any time a woman is hitting the stumps to tell women that they should stay home . . . well, she's not at home!
>
> I felt that the women's movement was saying that what I was doing wasn't worthwhile. I had a persistent sense of guilt, that I ought to be in some professional job and at the same time that I ought to be at home with the girls. I'd get involved in a job or project, and then I couldn't handle it so I'd get out of it, and then I'd get convinced again that I should be doing something else.

> **Wendy:** The women's movement has unsettled me more than anything else. I'm at home full-time with our children. I ask myself now and then, Am I really being fair to myself? Is this

important work, important enough to pursue full-time?

I have friends and people I admire greatly who are doing the feminist thing. They have important careers and nice families. And they make me wonder if I should be doing more.

Judith: The women's movement has made it very difficult for me. I find myself having to defend being at home—being a mom. People ask, "Do you work?" I say, "No." If I say, "Yes, I work because I am a homemaker with three children," it sounds like I'm being defensive or putting on airs. But I do feel defensive, sometimes.

The problem is, simply, that there are people, my husband included, who do not think that staying home with children is work. That's where the women's movement makes it difficult for me.

My husband expected me to have a career. He married a college graduate who was going to work.

We never really discussed this beforehand. I assumed that, because his mother was a homemaker, he would think that was the right thing for me to do when we had children. I kept my job through the first and second pregnancies, and then just had to give it up with our third child. He doesn't like this. I think he feels cheated. When the bills arrive he says, "I sure could use some help paying these off." And every time he says that, I feel like three big cement blocks have been placed on my back, and I'm just sinking into the ground.

When I was growing up, it was the women who worked outside the home who had to defend themselves. But now it's the mothers who stay home who have to defend themselves. The women's movement has turned everything around.

Even with the "freeing up" that was supposed to come with the women's movement, I don't feel free to explore and find out who I am. There are certain things that are expected of me—certain roles that I have to fulfill—and I don't feel that I can be anything besides that. All this talk that we're supposed to have come a long way—no, we haven't. There are new things that are expected of us now, but it all boils down to the same old thing, which is that we must do what is expected.

I feel split down the middle. Society is telling me to get a job and make something of my life; my mother is telling me to stay home with my children; my husband is saying he needs me to work so we can pay the bills. I have no freedom to do what I think is right. There are so many people giving their input as to what they think I should do with my life, that I'm distracted from figuring it out for myself.

I would be content to stay at home for a long time if I got more support. The only support I get for being a housewife is from insurance men! They put value on the work I do so that they can talk us into more life insurance.

Linda: Feminism has contributed to a more relaxed view in a very positive way. But there's a difference between shattering stereotypes that are culturally based—like shaving your legs—and shattering those that have to do with who we truly are as women. What I'm seeing in feminism today is a rejection of heterosexuality, which wipes out the truth of what our bodies were meant to be. I can't support that.

Tricia: My dad thought I was a big women's libber. A couple of my brothers still feel that way—but it's just because I haven't become a farm wife, and I work, and I don't live my life as they've seen women do it in the past.

I get very annoyed when a woman is being discriminated against in any way, and I'm willing to speak up about it. I can't say that I'd feel this way if it hadn't been for the influence of the women's movement.

I'm annoyed that the average woman still makes only sixty-four cents to the average working man's dollar. Or is it up to seventy cents? I find that amazing. Now that I'm working in higher education, I've discovered that more and more women are getting into my profession at my level because colleges and universities can't afford (or won't pay) the kind of salaries that attract qualified men.

Was it easier for women to fulfill their role in the family and society when the options were fewer? Is there less disappointment if a little girl raised to be, say, a farm wife, is never presented with other choices, never sees women doing anything different, and never has the opportunity to explore other possibilities? My suspicion is that even severe hardship is dealt with more successfully when expectations are firmly set by tradition. But our present generation will never know for sure.

One woman stated the situation well: "A lot of us were married under 'the old covenant.' We went into marriage with traditional views about our role, and our husbands were in agreement with us. But you add to this the turmoil of the sixties and seventies, the women's movement, the self-actualization quest, and you come up with problems. Those assumptions that were mutually held going into marriage need to be examined and evaluated on a continual basis."

GETTING AN EDUCATION

The widespread opportunity and encouragement for women to obtain higher education has had a big impact on our lives. We know that a woman of the younger generation is more likely to obtain a college degree and to put her learning to use in the marketplace than her mother was.

But that's a generalization. **Dorcas** is in her mid-seventies, and her story shows the folly of stereotyping a generation:

> I can't remember when I didn't look forward to my career. I didn't think of marriage as a primary goal. I wanted to do something on my own, to fulfill my call to ministry. In those days, you didn't have a career and marriage simultaneously; you had to choose one or the other. I couldn't bear to think of going right into marriage without this time on my own.
>
> My mother and father were always very supportive of me; they always said that I could do anything. My mother had had a career before she got married. I could be a lawyer, a professor, a doctor—they felt I *could*.
>
> They always made me think I was intelligent. They treated me as though I *was* intelligent.
>
> Education was important to my parents. When I left a prestigious university I was attending to enroll in Bible school, they were pretty upset, thinking that it might be the end of my schooling. They wanted me to have a good degree. But I had the most tremendous feeling of peace and well-being when I went to Bible

school, because I knew absolutely that this was where my life was going. (I did take the "church secretary" course, which was kind of stupid!)

After I left Bible school, I re-enrolled in college and then became a home missionary to American Indians.

By the time I reached thirty, I realized that my prospects for marriage were dwindling. I decided that if I met someone who was interested in me and that I was attracted to, I wouldn't pull back. I had attained my goal of having a career.

I always thought I wouldn't mind being a housewife if it was a *choice*. It would be a *chapter* in my life—not my whole life.

It did indeed turn out to be a chapter in her life as her husband died at an early age and the education she had received was put to good use when she had to rebuild her life as a single mother and career woman.

Several women told of more traditional expectations:

Tricia: My mother was supportive of me going to college. I always had straight As, was class valedictorian, always had succeeded. I didn't want to be stuck on the farm, stuck in a town, working in a factory or something like that.

My father finished grade school only; my mom finished high school. I have four brothers, but I'm the only one who has a college degree. Because of this, my father thought I wanted to be a man. That's just the way he was. He wasn't one to be very encouraging; he didn't give me pats on the back.

Karen: I grew up in a small farming town. Women in that setting didn't need education and they didn't get it. Sometimes they would work, if their family had fallen on hard times or if their husbands didn't make enough money or if it was a family business where her work was really needed. None of the work was career-oriented.

I got engaged while I was in college, and my father's expectation was that I would quit school. Since I was going to be married, I wouldn't need a job, so I didn't need to continue with my education. And I did quit. It was just fine with me. I had no big career goals.

My husband, on the other hand, had different expectations. His parents were involved in a family business, and his mother worked even when she had to do it with a baby strapped to her back. So he looked at me after we were married and said, "You're not just going to sit around the house, are you? Go do something!" He was the one who pushed me to do more than I might have otherwise.

He didn't insist that I have a big career, but he thought that I should do something with the talents that I had been given. And eventually he saw to it that I finished my degree.

Indeed, other women who grew up on farms—where the division of labor and the roles of the farmer and farm wife are still very distinct—had little encouragement to pursue a college education. Tricia was called a "women's libber" (with all the negative connotations included) by her father because she wanted to go to college and get a professional job. (Mothers seemed to be more supportive than fathers in these situations.) Tricia, by the way, went on to graduate from college with high honors.

Theresa grew up in a traditional *urban* family, and her experience is similar to Tricia's and Karen's:

> Education was not a priority for girls in my family. Our family was upper-middle class, and my father owned several restaurants in Manhattan. When I said I wanted to go to college after high school, I was told that girls don't need to go to college. They'll get married.

"I Can't Afford to Quit Asking the Question"

Our freedom to choose has brought with it the need to evaluate and reevaluate our decisions on an ongoing basis. Even those who assume a "traditional" woman's role today do it on the basis of choice, which isn't exactly traditional!

June's story, which follows, is one of continual examination and evaluation. Married in the mid-sixties, she tells of her early expectations for adult life and the eventual outcome.

> I expected that I would get married, have children, raise them in a family situation like my own (working father, stay-at-home mother), that I would live in a town (as opposed to a city), and that I would have the same support from the local church that my family did.
>
> My parents and all their friends were very involved in the church; it was the center of our social life. There were many adults in the church who played a big part in my life, as role models, as people who could explain the Christian faith and show how it was lived.
>
> I expected to have this, myself, when I was grown. I expected a lot of security and stability.

Did you pursue this kind of life?

Yes, somewhat. I got a degree in teaching—
something that would fit in with raising a family.
I married a man from my church, and that was in
keeping with all the expectations. But things
started to change once we moved away from our
home town. I started teaching in an inner-city
school, Gil went to graduate school, and we became part of the radical social change of the late
sixties. My views broadened, and other influences—other than family and the local church I
grew up in—entered my life.

My husband was in graduate school, and I
was part of a wives' group that tackled intellec-
tually challenging issues. I was exposed to a different culture, had different friends and
opportunities, began reading the newspaper . . . I
became more politically aware and active.

When I was working at the inner-city school,
I saw, for the first time, women who had professional careers and who also had small children
and were making other arrangements for their
care. I hadn't had any exposure to that when I
was growing up; I didn't know of any mothers
who worked.

This was the beginning of a very gradual
education in women's rights and human rights.
Still, in the back of my mind was the idea that I
would have a family and that, when I did, I'd stay
home with the children.

When I decided to go to graduate school and
get an MBA, I came to the realization that I
could not depend on a spouse's personal and
career ambitions to satisfy my own. I needed to
address these for myself.

How has it worked out?

Professionally, I'm doing things that relieve my anxieties. I do not work for an institution that has mandatory retirement, I can work as long as I have clients who want to hire me. So that settles my issue of enforced non-productivity. And my earnings are a reflection of how much work I put into the job; they are not dictated by a government agency or school board. This gives me a sense of control over my own life and my future.

I have tried very hard to see that my children aren't paying the price for my own professional security. It's a question I have constantly in front of me. As I look at how my kids are developing and as I compare notes with other parents, I think that they are *not* paying the price. But I can't afford to quit asking the question. I have to keep asking myself, Are my children losing out because I am doing this?

Because of the kind of work I do, because of my situation, I don't have a lot of role models. In the generation before mine, there weren't many women living this kind of life.

It's taken its toll on me in terms of physical exhaustion. It takes a tremendous amount of stamina, and I get tired.

Marriage has not exactly lived up to my expectations—but I'm glad it didn't. As I see the problems that have arisen in the lives of those who have lived as appendages to their spouses, I'm glad that isn't my situation. Yet, it's a clear difference from what I expected.

"CLICK"

Kerri: I have a vivid memory from when I was eleven years old. It was a Saturday; I had climbed a tree outside our house. Because our house was in a little valley, climbing the tree gave me a street-eye-view of the rest of the neighbor-hood. I was climbing the tree because my mom was inside, cleaning the house, and she didn't want me tracking dirt across the kitchen floor, which had just been washed.

While I was in the tree, I saw a man who lived down the street get dropped off at his house. He had his tennis racquet, and he had his tennis clothes on; he had been out with his friend play-ing tennis.

And I thought, *I just don't think I can stand this. All the wives are inside mopping floors, and all the husbands are playing tennis this morning. Why did I have to be born a woman?*

It's not that I hated being female, but I hated what it implied about how I would have to live my life. I couldn't stand the idea of being a traditional wife and mother. That's when I first started thinking that I'd rather be a part of a "non-traditional" marriage, where I could have some freedom.

Kerri, at the age of eleven, heard a "click." She understood in an instant that there was some injustice in all (!) the wives scrubbing floors and all the hus-bands playing tennis. Click! She began to form a belief as a pre-teenager that is with her into her forties.

For **Ginger**, a similar belief came later, under dif-ferent circumstances, and gradually.

I thought I had to be a full-time mother when my kids were little, but now I see that I didn't. And everything I've ever said about mothers who weren't home for their kids—mothers who worked—I've had to eat it. Eat it for dinner. I take it all back.

The plain and simple truth in my life is that even though I was home with my kids before they were in school, I wasn't there for them. And it would have been far better if I'd just faced up to my own needs and gifts and callings instead of clinging to this single belief: that good mothers stay home.

The "symbiotic" mother in me wants to know the last time my kids peed, the last time they took a drink of water, and what book they're looking at right now. That's no kind of mother to have! Now that I have a life outside the home, my children have more of a life too.

I heard statements like this: "Just being at home, alone, with my kids and my nuclear family, isn't going to do it for me." And, "For me, working—even though I don't make very much money—gives me a sense of worth. I feel that I'm contributing something, and that I deserve more of a say in what happens in our family when I'm working."

Baloney!

The issue of worth seemed for many to be central to the issue. Many mothers I talked to who are now at home with their children or who were at the time their children were growing up asserted that it is absolutely worthwhile to do so. They describe a life of fulfillment deriving from their commitment to husband and children.

However, others, just as committed to this traditional role for themselves, questioned the whole issue of worth and fulfillment.

Katherine: I suppose it is possible for the woman to be the one who works and brings in the money to support the family, and the husband could stay home and be the glue that holds the family together, the nurturer. But I've never seen that happen. So, if we take as a given that the man is going to work outside the home and that he's pouring his energy into his job, then it is legitimate that the wife and mother has to be making the decisions that center around the home: getting the children where they need to go and guiding their decisions.

Whether it feels fulfilling or not?

Absolutely. We buy this myth that as Christians we're supposed to feel fulfilled. That's not in the Bible. Where did we get promised that we were going to have comfort and fulfillment? We get promised suffering and work, and not many are preaching about that.

Mothers think that once their children are in school, they don't need them so much. It is a milestone, but I don't think it's true that mothers aren't needed at home just because children are in school.

I came into marriage thinking that women had a *right* to work outside the home and that I had that same right. But now we don't talk about rights in our marriage. It's not a word we use.

Ingrid: In countering the women's movement, the Christian world has bombarded us with propaganda about how wonderful it is to stay home, how fulfilling it is to be a mother. Well, I have yet to see it happen. To me, it's not fulfilling. It's just plain hard work. And I have yet to see in Scripture where it says that motherhood is fulfilling. The Christian writers say it will be, though.

Bridgette: I wonder if it isn't a long-lost art to enjoy your children, to be happy in your home, to be hospitable to others. There don't seem to be any points given for this sort of thing, although lately I've been sensing that other women are finding this kind of life worthwhile and enjoyable. Every now and then you'll see an article in a women's magazine where the writer admits that the babysitter she was looking for turned out to be herself. Being out in the world, pushing and striving in that arena, isn't for everyone.

THE "S" WORD

In my recollection, the publication of the book *The Total Woman* by Marabel Morgan brought the issue of submission to the fore. Before then, the biblical dimensions of the issue had been either accepted without question or ignored without hesitation. But Morgan's provocative approach to the marriage dynamic tended to draw women (and men) to one side or the other: A) the submissive wife who gets what she wants by letting hubby be the boss and cheerfully inspiring him to greater love and generosity through deference, or B) the assertive wife who claims parity under God and faces the world as the equal of her mate, and woe to them who say otherwise.

These are caricatures of the two opposite points of view. But I do remember being very upset for quite a long time about the whole issue of submission. It began in high school when the boys in our church youth group started razzing us about our "inferiority" to them. They knew we didn't respect them much at the time but looked forward to the day when perhaps some of us would be married (God forbid!) to some of them, and then we'd *have* to answer their beck and call.

In all honesty, the developing male ego being what it is, I don't think I've overstated their attitude.

One woman in our church, listening to my tearful protestations over the unfairness of it all, remarked through clenched teeth, "Yeah? Well, I submit to every man who loves me as much as Christ loves the church." I got the message, but somehow I wasn't consoled.

The issue of submission has, on and off, occupied my thoughts—and I found that it was a concern for many of the women I talked to. So if you stutter when uttering the "S" word, consider yourself in good—and sympathetic—company!

For even where there's a willingness to submit to one's husband and a desire for the husband to assume the spiritual leadership of the family, the particulars of working that out are often troublesome:

> **Darlene:** Spiritually, this is a problem for me. I'd rather that Nate be the head of the household, but my personality is such that I run the show. It's very frustrating to sit back and wait for him to think of something that's already been on my mind for quite some time.
>
> For instance, perhaps the kids are bored and I get the idea that we could all go out to ShowBiz, or to the zoo, or maybe even take a weekend trip. If I bring it up, then Nate will feel bad that *he* didn't think of it. But if I *don't* bring up the idea, then he sure won't think of it on his own, and everyone continues to sit around the house being bored.

Sue Ellen: *The Total Woman* inspired me. Nowadays, no one refers to that book without making a joke of it. But years ago, when I read it, I was a new wife—I thought, yes, yes, yes! I never thought that her approach was manipulative. I thought that her philosophy of being organized, having your life together, being the kind of person that your husband would like to come home to . . . I liked that attitude.

Four women whose definitions of submission might have been "to give in to what your husband thinks is best" described major disappointments with the concept as they put it into practice.

Marilyn: For several years, Donald was a minister in the denomination that we have now officially parted from. I was very unhappy in the minister's wife's role, especially since I was uncomfortable with the doctrines of that denomination. But I thought that this was a time that I should submit, that this was just the sort of situation where the wife should do what the husband thinks is right.

Eventually, Donald left the ministry with that denomination because he knew I was unhappy. This caused a huge upheaval between him and his mother. Years earlier, she had moved from one part of the country that she liked to another part of the country she hated, because that's what her husband wanted to do. The fact that I found my situation difficult and that Donald gave in to me sort of invalidated her own decision.

She believes women ought to be where their husbands want them to be. She did it, and when I *didn't*, I became the corruptor of her son. It hasn't raised my stock with the in-laws.

As it turns out, Don is just as happy now as I am. He doesn't lay it on me that we made the change.

Meredith: Making a major decision when we were not in agreement, and we *knew* we weren't, has been the biggest stress in our marriage.

What was the decision?

It was to move into this house. I didn't want to, and he did.

But you're here.

But it was a big mistake. I'm not sure what kind of choice I had. Carl would present me with papers that needed my signature and I signed. I didn't feel good about it, but I fell back on, "Wives, submit to your husbands."

There's an excellent book entitled *Lovers: Whatever Happened to Eden.* In it, the author points out that there is a common fallacy operating among Christians in that many people look at the curse that is laid on man and woman after the fall in Genesis (the woman is going to be under her husband's authority), and they idolize that curse as what marriage *should* be like.

Instead, we should go back to Eden and to the way things were before sin, where Adam and Eve were "co-regents" of everything. This is what we should be striving for. We should strive for what God *intended*, not be satisfied with what our sin brings. I think that if I had read that book before this house issue came up, I wouldn't have gone along with Carl's insistence that we buy it. I wouldn't have signed the papers that I signed.

It is cold comfort to realize, now, that I was probably right about this house and that Carl was wrong. Cold comfort. The house has been nothing but trouble since we moved in—it's a disaster. But we're stuck with it.

Robin: When I married Richard, I thought I would be a "good wife." I'd cook for him, wash his clothes, support him in whatever he wanted to do. That didn't last long! I very much wanted to give him the headship of the home, when we got married. That didn't last long, either!

What happened?

I found, quite soon, that I hated taking full responsibility for the home and family. Even though I took it on willingly at first, it became a tremendous burden.

A lot of my frustration was that there was never any positive feedback from anyone in the house. My whole job was in the house, and I got no respect or appreciation for what I did. In addition to that, Rich had become my whole life. He was my pastor, my teacher, my husband, my children's father . . . he had such authority over me.

I got no respect for the work I did. My husband got lots of respect, and my children did too. But not me.

Once I was able to verbalize this to Richard, he was very understanding. He didn't think I should have to shoulder it all alone. At first, he "helped out." I was grateful for that, but it took quite a while, and took a real redefining of roles for us to come to the place where the work was really shared.

Diane: The women's movement was confusing for me. Everywhere I went it was the same thing: "I just have to be myself, and George won't let me be myself and I'm just going to have to leave."

After struggling with all this for a couple of years, and after hearing other women struggle with it, I realized that I needed to make a decision.

I remember going to a retreat with women from all over the state, and everyone was saying this same thing: I hate men, I hate my husband, I have to be myself and George . . . he won't let me be myself.

Well, there was one woman at this retreat who was always kind of by herself and on the fringe. She stood up on the last day and said, "You know, I am really anxious to go home and see my husband, whom I love very much."

And I thought, *That's really neat. Maybe Clifford isn't letting me be who I want to be, but surely there's some love there; there's some love left in the world between men and women.*

I made a very conscious decision—and I talked to a friend about it to solidify it, so that I would stick with it. I was either going to divorce Clifford and "be a person," like everyone was talking about, or become a submissive woman. When I thought about my family, I realized that the best choice was to become a submissive woman. I didn't want to hurt my children—I've been through my parents' divorce—and I realized that as they approached adolescence and their teenage years, things would be a whole lot easier for them if they had a father—someone to be there for them, even to put them through college. It was a pragmatic decision.

So I became a submissive wife. It was survival.

What did this mean on a practical level?

It meant learning how to live and survive in peace and getting as much my way as I could, without causing a lot of commotion. I would have to calculate: Clifford will only let me have my way on this many things within the next week, so I'd better decide what those things are going to be.

I gave up some things for myself so that the girls could have more.

Material things?

Personhood things. Bobbie needed a lot of freedom at that time, and I could buy some freedom for her by taking less for myself. I had stamina enough to fight for what the girls needed, but not enough left over to get what I needed.

It meant a lot of manipulation and very little confrontation.

Looking back, how do you grade it?

As a way to live? If I had to make the same decision, I wouldn't do anything differently. I know it wasn't healthy for *me*. After several years of this I began having all sorts of physical symptoms, and I think that they're related to the stress that this submission caused. But I don't see any other way that I could have done it. Clifford is just too strong of a person for me.

I got plenty of blank looks when I asked about submission, too. Some women had never entertained the notion at any level, and others had never questioned it. The issue seemed decidedly settled for those who had been married for some time. "I don't think about it any more," said one woman. "It makes me tired. When I hear people discussing it and grappling with it, I think, 'Oh, just forget it. Relax—it'll work itself out.'" But for some people, it obviously is a big issue.

> **Wendy:** When I first got married, I was really hung up on the hierarchy of God, man, woman—the Bill Gothard thing. I tried to push Stu into taking an assertive role in our marriage, being the spiritual head. I'm not sure I knew what a spiritual leader was. Maybe I thought he should insist on and lead devotions every day. I don't know. I would go around and around with him—what did it mean for him to be the spiritual leader in our family?
>
> The whole submission issue is so far down on the list of Stu's and my priorities that we don't think about it at all anymore. It's so much more important to figure out how to be a Christian, how to live the Christian life—submission is a minor issue in comparison.
>
> I can't really tell you what happened, or why it ceased to be an issue for us. I do see now that it's a canned idea; a box that may make it easier to *feel* you're doing the right thing for the Lord, but something that's not necessarily true.

MY MODEL, CAROLINE INGALLS

A day doesn't go by but that I think of Ma Ingalls—the mother of Laura Ingalls Wilder who wrote the *Little House* books. I read those books when I was a child—all of them, many times. As a little girl, I might have identified with Laura or Mary, the daughters, but it was their mother, Caroline Ingalls, who left the greatest impression on me.

Caroline Ingalls was, I believe, married to a madman. "Pa" in the books wasn't a bit like Michael Landon in the television version of *Little House on the*

Prairie. Pa Ingalls was a restless pioneer, and he drew his family into his ceaseless quest for opportunity and independence. Laura Ingalls writes that Pa moved the family from the woods to the prairie when the family began to hear "the ringing thud of an ax which was not Pa's ax, or the echo of a shot that did not come from his gun." The Big Woods were getting crowded!

Ma followed Pa, of course. She did her best to provide softness to his rough edges; she protected the family when he was away. Such were her homemaking skills that she could feed her growing family on what little Pa could trap or shoot, and the produce she raised from her garden. She could dry fruits and vegetables, salt the meat, dress the chickens, bake bread and simply make do, with little more than nothing.

She was a strong woman, and her strength and courage made a lasting impression on me. Every day, as I confront some challenge or step back to appreciate some modern convenience, I think to myself, "What would Ma Ingalls have thought if she could see the price of this cotton dress?" or "What could Ma Ingalls make for supper with what I've got here in the cupboard?" or "Just think how Ma Ingalls' life would have been different with only the simple luxury of running water—or a washer and dryer." Ma is with me always.

When my mind is wrestling over the issues of traditional versus innovative living styles—as it often does—I remember Caroline Ingalls. If I am tempted to think that she was the epitome of the traditional pioneer woman, I must remember that during her lifetime there was no traditional role for pioneer women—that's why they called them pioneers! Everything was new. The skills and mores of city living in the East were not directly transferable to the wild and woolly West. Those who could not adapt, who were weak or overcome, returned to their homes or died along the way. The Oregon Trail was littered with their graves. The strong ones, those who survived the experience, were forced to evaluate each new situation and improvise solutions to problems they had never confronted before. They lived in times of change and turmoil, as we do today.

And as I look at Caroline Ingalls' life, I realize that when we talk about whether or not a woman should stay at home with her husband and children or join the nation's work force; whether she should submit or assert; whether she should seek self-fulfillment or self-denial . . . there's more to being a woman than simply accepting or rejecting the expectations of family, community, church, or self. There is something more.

TERRI'S STORY

At the age of nineteen, Terri married a man eleven years her senior, and shortly thereafter moved to his family's farm in Canada. The high school cheerleader became a farm wife, mother and, eventually, minister's wife.

My husband asked God for a wife. He prayed about it. And when he found himself being drawn to me, he took that as an answer to his prayer. I was a teenybopper when he started to court me. I was dating another guy, a nice Christian fellow. But Vic had "the inside story from the Lord," as he put it. He didn't want to bother himself with searching for a wife; he left that up to the Lord.

I wanted the Lord to choose my husband. I was always hearing about that sort of thing, though I hadn't given much thought to it myself. I was nineteen.

At the time, I was having fun with my friends and was very active in the church activities. Victor was a good friend of my father's. I just didn't think about him much until he began to ask me out, and then told me he believed God had chosen me for him. We first started seeing each other around Easter, and were married the following September. It was a short courtship.

Soon you moved out of the city onto your husband's family farm, which was vacant.

That seemed like a really neat thing to me, to leave the city I'd grown up in, move away from my parents, and move to this beautiful farm in Canada. Vic had told me about the lakes, and the trees, and how beautiful it was—and I was really excited to go.

But it wasn't what I expected. The house was nearly without paint, heated with a wood-burning stove, had an antique kitchen, a sagging porch, no closets, little space, peeling old linoleum on the floors . . . I realized then that I was going to have to deal with my expectations. I felt lost. There was a lot of disappointment.

About that time we started having children—two babies, thirteen months apart. For a long time, we had only one vehicle. Vic needed it to look for work, so I was bound to the house. We didn't have much money, but I didn't feel that I could do outside work because I was pregnant.

I fought being depressed. I had no friends, we lived so far away from everything and everyone. There were some people who came to the house, and they did try to relate to me. But I stayed to myself. People wanted to get in, but I wouldn't let them.

When I was depressed, I lay in bed in the mornings. Maybe I could hear that the baby was awake, and I'd say, "Vic, why should I get up? I know what's out there—there's work out there! I don't want to do work." Sometimes he'd almost have to pull me out of bed; at least, he'd have to pull the covers off the bed so I'd get up. He'd force me to get up.

You've gone along with your husband on a pretty wild adventure: making a go of a farm.

There was a time when I told Vic, "I don't want to be here any more." Life was too hard. I was lonely, I was depressed, I wanted to live in a city.

He said, "That's fine; I'm going to stay here, and you can go." That was my option, if I was really serious about getting out of the situation.

I'm not real big on divorce, so I stayed.

Was there a turning point for you?

Yes. One night we just sat down and Vic said, "Okay, we're going to get some paper out and make a list. On this side you write everything you're seeing that's negative in your life, and on the other side I want you to put down all the good things."

So I did. The negative side was long; there were all kinds of things that I thought weren't right. On the positive side there were just a few measly little things that I made up.

He looked at that, and then he said, "Terri, you're going to have to find something bigger than yourself."

For some reason that did something for me. I realized that I needed to start getting out of my own situation and try to help other people. I needed to find even just one little positive thing that I could do from my own house, with kids.

So I started to ask people over. I think it was the Lord who made that one little step I took turn into something worthwhile, because I began to have success with friendships and hospitality.

Before that time, I didn't want to have people in the house, period. It was such a job: get the kids in order, cook food, clean the house. It would take a week to do that.

When you decided to have people in your home, did it take a week to get the house in order, or did you just have them in anyway?

I decided to go to the work. I thought the preparations were important. In fact, this was one area of disagreement between Vic and me. He was out in the community all day, and he thought that it was just fine to invite people over on a moment's notice, without consulting me as to whether or not I felt ready for it, regardless of what shape the house was in.

I also needed to get prepared emotionally. Sometimes people would come over and I'd just be tight inside. I didn't want to be with people.

I began to see all this as a challenge for me to get out of myself.

It was hard, but I began to have friendships of my own that weren't connected to Victor. I got out of his shadow somewhat.

Do you continue to be depressed?

Not in the same way. I've grown through my experience with depression, and I've learned that when I feel it coming on I don't have to give in to it, to let it become a pattern that rules my life. I don't want to do that any more. I know that Christ is in me, and I do have the power to resist all those negative feelings.

THE TEACHING OF OLDER WOMEN

I was overwhelmed by our house: small, no closets, hard to keep clean, all that. I needed to learn how to get organized and keep things neat.

I prayed. I told God that he could help me with this, and that I wanted him to.

Shortly after that when I was at church, an older lady came up to me and said that the night before she had been praying for me, and the Lord told her that she should come and help me with my house. She was real embarrassed to tell me that, but I wasn't. Thank you! Thanks!

This was a neat old lady, who was used to carrying water into the house and heating it over a stove—old-fashioned housekeeping. She had worked in the barn a lot. She knew how to work hard at being a farm wife and how to be efficient. She knew it was important.

She told me she would come over once a week to help me. I figured I had to clean up the house first. And I thought that the last place she'd go to would be the refrigerator, so I got busy in the kitchen because I didn't want it to be too filthy; I wanted to get it neatened up a little bit.

So she came—she brought lunch for everyone, because she wanted it to be simple. And then she said, "Well, I've found that it's almost always good to start with the refrigerator. If your refrigerator is organized, you can find a place to put your food." I was so embarrassed—here she was pulling out old wilted heads of lettuce, moldy cheese and sour milk. It was pretty comical.

In a period of weeks, she had really helped me a lot. We went from room to room, figuring out how each one could be better. She worked with me, washing dishes and dusting and sorting. Vic got inspired, too; he built some simple shelves in a bedroom that was already stacked to the ceiling with junk, and we made that room into a closet with shelves and rods for hanging up our clothes.

She never made me feel dumb. She'd say, "Oh, well, I had to teach my girls to do all this—I'm still teaching them!" And she encouraged me: "At least with you, Terri, once I tell you something you remember it."

One day, I sat down and wrote her a card telling her how much I appreciated her help. She didn't come back after that; she figured that her work was done and that she'd done what she could.

I've tried to remember a lot of what she said. It was just like in the Bible, where it talks about how the older women should teach the younger women. She was a turning point in my life. She's still very close to me. And whenever I can get ahold of an old lady who's experienced a lot, I want to learn whatever she can teach me.

We were having a lot of problems with our children when they were real small. It was obvious to everyone at church; I was in the nursery all the time because they'd scream if I left them alone. I'd sit in the nursery and cry. If Stephen didn't get his way, he'd scream until he passed out. I was desperate, and I hinted to other people that I needed help, that I didn't know what to do. But nobody said anything.

Then one day a lady from church came over to our house. She sat Victor and me down at the kitchen table and said, "Your children are out of control because you're not disciplining them."

We started following through with our discipline, which we had not been doing at all up to that point.

How was it up to that point, exactly?

If the kids wanted something, and we said no, then they'd scream and cry and run around the house and finally we'd give in and give them what they had asked for.

We did this from the very beginning. When I was nursing Mary (our second child) I never felt like putting her down, getting up, and following through on Stephen's (our older child's) discipline. I had no desire or willingness to be an authority in my own house. So it was a pattern that continued until we had two children who were really out of our control.

And how did you change things then?

We decided that we wouldn't tell them to do anything that we weren't willing to follow through on. And we would follow through until they had done what they were told to do.

So, instead of saying halfheartedly, "I'm going to get you if you keep doing that . . . this is your third warning!" and then letting the third warning come and go without any consequences for their disobedience, we started disciplining them right away. No more warnings. Sometimes it was like a surprise attack.

Almost immediately, we started enjoying our children for the first time. It was really strange. We could go to a restaurant and public places without embarrassment. People started inviting us over, and we had pleasant times.

Give me a for-instance.

They were always wanting to eat things that we didn't want them to eat: candy, pop. Stephen would ask, I'd say no. He'd start screaming, arch his back—and you can't do anything with a child who's arched his back: you can't dress him, or hold him, or anything. Sometimes he'd even pass out.

So I didn't pay any attention to that. He'd carry on and carry on, and still he didn't get what he wanted. There were times I'd ignore him, times I'd give him a swat because I felt that he needed it. Maybe I'd send him to his room—but not for any longer than I could stand it. I wouldn't threaten to put him in there for an hour, and then let him come out after two minutes because I was tired of hearing his screams. I'd send him to his room for five minutes, because that was a reasonable amount of time.

I'm sure that he was wanting to find some limits all along, and I wasn't giving them to him. It wasn't too long before we got to the point that I could tell the kids, "Put the book away, don't tear the pages," and they'd do it. They knew that if they disobeyed, there would be consequences, and that I wasn't afraid to impose those consequences. And it would happen right away.

CULTURAL DIFFERENCES

Did you think you'd marry someone white or someone black?

Black. Always. If there's a question-and-answer time when I get to heaven, I'm going to ask why I'm married to a white man. God's got to have a reason for doing this to me.

I've told Victor, "Honey, there are so many nice white girls who would have died to marry you and live on this farm with you . . . why me?" They wouldn't have had to adapt like I've had to adapt. I'm the only black person for miles and miles around.

Has the adjustment been harder for you because you are black?

Well, probably it's mostly because I was raised in town. Nobody here has bothered me about being black; in a way, maybe it's been a benefit to me. I'm unusual.

As my children are getting older, I would like them to be more acquainted with black culture. That side of me is something that I have always loved, but that I've had to put aside in my life. I miss my black family and my black friends.

It's a different way of being. Every now and then I see it coming out in my kids, and I know it's something in their blood that they really aren't getting in touch with because they aren't around other blacks. I suppose it's something they see in me.

When we're with my family, or my black friends, they love the blackness of these people. They realize, too, that there's a way to act and relate when they're with black people that is different than the way they act and relate around their white relatives and friends.

Victor and I have both grown. Through those years when I would have loved to leave the farm, he wasn't willing to do that. His heels were dug in pretty deep. But now if I wanted to leave the farm he would take my feelings seriously. Then we'd pray about it; and I feel confident that we'd be in agreement about what was the right thing to do.

I think that we are in the right place now. Perhaps I had a sense of that all along. To escape would have meant that I was running away from God, too—not just the situation I was in. I've found there was grace for me if I would apply it.

You know how it is to have a feeling that even though something is difficult, it's still the right thing to do, and God is working through it? That's the way it's been with me. There's something in me that doesn't want to be too far out on a limb. Maybe with my husband, but certainly not with the Lord.

Through all these different things, I've had the sense that I am in the right place, and that there was grace for me if only I'd apply it. I found that to be true.

CHAPTER FOUR

Parents and Children

Judith: One of my warmest memories from my childhood is coming home from morning kindergarten, and my mother—just to make it a special day—had laid a checkered tablecloth on the floor and made macaroni and cheese (which was my childhood favorite) and I got to eat lunch in front of the TV and watch "I Love Lucy." On the floor. It was wonderful.

Another time, we were driving past the local potato chip company, and my mother stopped and asked them if my brothers and I could have a tour through the plant. And it was okay. I can still remember what it was like to eat those warm potato chips.

There were these special memories, and I love them. This is the kind of mother I want to be.

Karen: My mother is my spiritual role model. I remember coming down in the morning and seeing her at the dining room table having her devotions. She really lived the fruits of the spirit. If someone said something unkind about another person, it was my mother who would always say, "Perhaps she'd had a hard time of it," or "Maybe he wasn't feeling well when he did that." She never raised her voice at me. She set a great example. Even though I never wanted my life to be like her life, I've always wanted to be the kind of person she is.

These two women were among a minority who spoke of their mothers in completely positive terms. And only one woman had completely unreserved praise for her father: "My self-esteem came from my father. I got so much of everything from him, I really didn't need another man. My husband loved my dad, too. I know so many women who have poor relationships with their father, or false relations, or no relationship at all. And they have low self-esteem. I got all of mine from my father."

I asked women to tell me what their childhood families were like, and what they got from their parents in the way of expectations for their own families, especially for their parenting. To tell the truth, I was saddened by their responses. Of course, to be fair we'd have to get the parents' point of view as well. So it could be argued that the stories that follow are one-sided, and I'm sure they are.

But to the extent that they *perceived* their parents to be unloving, manipulative, distant, or otherwise inadequate we get a picture of parents who have failed, children who were neglected in some way (perhaps abused), relationships that withered.

There is healing, though. Many women I talked to—like Rose, Audrey and Nedra—have been able to objectively, not bitterly, identify their parents' shortcomings and forgive those deficiencies. (Read ahead to "Helen's Story" on page 245 for an inspiring account of healing and forgiveness, child to mother.)

It's not easy; it takes minute-by-minute effort. But many are making that effort and succeeding in creating a better atmosphere in their own families.

Rose: My home life when I was growing up was schizophrenic. My parents professed one thing on a spiritual level, but it didn't happen on the practical level. Decisions were reached, and the reason would be expressed as, "Because it's God's will, we're doing this." But I never believed that. I think God was invoked to legitimize something that they wanted to do because it was convenient or suited their plans.

My parents were emotionally out of control. Home was noisy and scary and angry. It takes many acts of will each day to keep my own home from being this way. I can decide to do things the way my mother and father did, or I can choose something different.

My hope is that in my life there will be cohesive agreement between spiritual and practical matters. I'm trying to create an atmosphere with my children in which they understand that they have value and personhood beyond what they accomplish or how they act. I'm trying to create an atmosphere of peace—emotional peace. And it's hard for me to do that, because I don't feel that I have a lot of peace myself.

Audrey: My mother didn't give me a good model of the nurturing mother. Consequently, I just made my own rules with my children; I had no preconceived notions.

I figure I'm going to teach my kids how to survive in this world because they'll need to know that. They do a lot of things for themselves and take care of a lot of their own problems. I guess I'm not the nurturing mommy. I'll walk with them through their problems, but I'm not very good at carrying them.

Nedra: I have some anxiety about having a daughter. I don't know if I could be a good mother to a girl because I certainly have some hurt about the way my mother treated me. I would like to give a daughter good things, but I don't know if I have good things to give. I'm leery about passing on some of the creepy things my mother handed to me. And in some ways, I'm like her.

I've tried to approach my parents on some unfinished issues, but they refuse to discuss them with me. Their response is: "We did the best we could, and that's good enough." It's probably true that they did the best they could. But in certain cases their best wasn't good enough. And I wonder why they can't admit that; it would really be so helpful to me. Instead, they say, "We did the best we could. There's something wrong with you if you think that's not enough."

If my son comes to me at the age of eighteen or twenty and says, "I had this need when I was younger, and you ignored it," I'm prepared to respond: "Yes, I'm really sorry that I didn't get it right. Is there anything I can do now to help you?" I'm preparing myself to be willing to admit my failures.

Ginger is a professional woman in her late thirties, the mother of three, who tells of the many expectations she had for motherhood and how some of those expectations were met while others were not.

There is nothing with more potential than a newborn baby. When I was pregnant and when I gave birth, I thought about everything those kids could be and do.

But then as they grew older—it's a daily thing, really—their limitations become more apparent. Maybe this one won't be very affectionate, that one isn't too smart, my own daughter will have stringy hair! They go from being anything to being something.

I brought into motherhood as many expectations as there are expectations. I went into it spiritually open. I've never been more connected, mystically, with God and the universe than I was through the birth of my kids.

Childbirth—it was like war. Men make their war stories romantic because it's a confrontation with death. That's how birth was for me—a confrontation with death. I stared fear and danger in the face and came out alive; I was invincible.

I also became one with my children. I was totally unified with them; who they were and the love I felt for them was all of a piece. This is called symbiosis, and is intensified co-dependence. It's not good.

Explain.

When they cried, it killed me; I couldn't stand it. I had to provide for their every physical and emotional need. I lost myself. I breathed with my kids, I lived their lives. The experience had to be perfect.

When my oldest was six months old, she had surgery for cancer. By that time, I was so hooked into her life that I went through the valley with her. I lived it as if it were my own disease.

I became very bored and then very depressed. One time I cried for days and days. I was mourning the loss of the mothering fantasy. It was

89

important for me to do this, to give up this life where I *was* my child.

I really bought into the "earth mother" thing. Absolutely. I bought the image of it, from wearing earth tones to baking bread. I would be the strong woman who nurtured herself through her work in the family.

Then I came to the place where I wondered, "What's wrong with me?" because it wasn't working. I became bored. I was a crab.

Our first child was a girl. When I was pregnant with our second, I was absolutely convinced that I was carrying a boy. When *she* was born, I went into depression, right on the delivery table. It was such a shock; I had no idea that the baby would be a girl. I wondered what was wrong; I suppose I thought I could control her sex.

I wonder if our second has scars from all that. I don't think our bonding was "clean." I am really ashamed of the whole thing, but it *did* happen. I held back with her; there was guilt between us. I asked her forgiveness for my parenting failures when she was an infant; I had to.

One Big Surprise After Another

Darlene: When I had babies I didn't ever think that they might become teenagers and that I'd have to let them go. I only thought about how nice it would be to have a baby, a cute little kid running around.

And marriage! Who thinks about her husband going bald, getting a tummy, producing dirty underwear that has to be washed? If we thought about these things, we'd never get married. And we wouldn't have children either, probably.

Do you know what I hate? I hate it when someone in our house gets sick . . . especially if there are body fluids involved. My friend Billie admits that cleaning up after her husband's stomach flu took every bit of love she had for him. It's something you just don't plan for when you're picking out china and silverware patterns.

Sue Ellen: I didn't think that I would have difficult kids. I figured that if I did everything right they'd turn out fine. But the conflicts, the stress! I had no idea these problems with our teenagers were coming. Well, thank goodness I didn't! Thank goodness! I'm glad I was ignorant.

Linda: I pictured having kids the way I remembered my early childhood: building towers with blocks, reading books, sitting on the couch playing with dolls. I don't remember a lot of big problems. I've had times of extreme frustration with my kids where I've said, "This is not the way kids are supposed to act. This is not how mothering is supposed to feel. This is far too hard; it feels too impossible for it to be natural or right. Why aren't they playing on the couch? Why are they destroying it instead?"

The women who still have children at home all confessed, in their own ways, that motherhood was turning out to be one surprise after another. From the surprise of having a child with stringy hair to the surprise of having a Caesarean birth ("I never thought I'd have to be cut up to have kids!"), to the surprise of being less than perfect ("Because I taught preschool before I had my own children, I thought I knew what to expect of myself—I thought I'd be a perfect mother"), I heard a veritable litany of astonishment.

> **Tanya:** Motherhood? It's all been a surprise. I had no idea it would be so fatiguing, especially the first couple of years.
>
> I can look at Sheila and tears of joy will come to my eyes because of something precious she's done. And then she'll act like a pill, and I'll want to wring her neck. The emotions she pulls out of me!
>
> I remember walking into church when Sheila was just a couple months old, and everyone would gather around us, and be happy that we had this baby, and say things like, "Isn't mother-hood wonderful?" And I asked myself, "What am I missing?" The first six months were not won-derful; they were awful. I was nursing her every couple of hours, around the clock; my breasts were just raw; I wasn't getting sleep.

And while we're on the subject of the womanly art of breastfeeding . . .

> **Marsha:** I had this lovely picture of nursing my baby: how I'd cradle her in my arms, feed her from my body. Well, it was more like nursing an eggbeater than anything else. And that was the beginning of the crumbling of the wonderful plan I had for her life.
>
> I realized when she was born that she is a real person, and that she has legitimate preferences and those won't always coincide with the way I think things should be.
>
> **Melissa:** Nobody told me it would be so hard. And I think my two kids are as good as kids can be. One had colic, which isn't unusual, but I

found it very, very hard. She'd cry for hours; I'd walk her, and then get tired and sit down in a chair ever so slowly, not noticeable jerking or anything, but the minute my seat hit the chair, she'd start screaming again.

I thought motherhood would be more automatic; I'd just *know* what to do. But it takes a lot of thought, a lot of physical and emotional energy.

And you know what really ticks me off? There are no rules. Everybody does it a different way; each book you read, each person you talk to has a different point of view, a different philosophy of parenting.

I WANT MY TROPHY!

That's right: no rules, and no trophies either.

Steve and I joke about the "Mother of the Year" and "Father of the Year" awards. After accomplishing some particularly brilliant and daring act of parenting, we can be heard to exclaim triumphantly to our spouse and children, "Just remember this when the Parent-of-the-Year Committee calls!"

Is it so much to ask? Shouldn't there be some tangible and formal recognition for the dad who fixes, on the average, three broken toys per week and acts out elaborate Superhero adventures with his sons? ("Okay, Lex, we're taking you to the Hall of Justice!") What is there for the mom who co-chairs the PTA Book Fair and makes pancakes in the shapes of rabbits and cats? (Yes, I do.) How about a statue of a pot-bellied woman with her hand in a bronze toilet? I'd like such a prize.

Short of that, I do expect some sort of reward for the job I'm doing. After all, it takes a lot of hard work and sacrifice; it's easily twice as hard as any paid job I've ever had. It's very important; the responsibility is fierce and demands my very best.

Some mothers are seeing rewards in their job of raising children: their kids are loving, respectful, and creative. These women are able to see their positive influence on the lives of their children. They found motherhood challenging and fulfilling. They made sacrifices for it, and found blessings. As one woman said, "I don't think I ever realized how much I would grow as a person because of becoming a parent. There is a lot of emphasis on how you can grow through a career, but not much on how women can grow through motherhood. I'm a different person, probably better, for being the mother of five children. I've learned how to cope with difficult situations."

Robin, the mother of four, was less exuberant:

> I thought motherhood would be much more rewarding. I thought that if you did a good job, if you raised them the way they should be raised, they would reward you. In some ways that's true; some of our children have rewarded us.
>
> But I thought if you raised your children properly, they'd be proper children. That's not true. There's so much that they're just born with. All of our children have grown up in the same house, with the same rules, the same parents, the same expectations. They're all different.

WHO'S RESPONSIBLE HERE?

The mother, that's who. In spite of the fact that it takes two to create a child, women were absolutely unanimous that when all the talk about shared parenting is over, when all the discussions over women's rights have finished, it's the mom who bears the greatest responsibility for the family.

> **Patricia:** Whether I like it or not, I'm the only one in this house who is there for everybody else. I need to be there cheerfully. It's a laying down of my life.

> **Marilyn:** I found Edith Schaeffer's books *The Hidden Art of Homemaking* and *What Is a Family?* very helpful. I realized that the family has potential, and someone jolly well better see to it that that potential isn't wasted.

> **Kristine:** I loved being pregnant; I liked the clothes and the pampering. But once I had the baby, I was depressed. A week after she was born, I thought, *Now I've done it. I've gone too far this time. I'm going to have this crying, squalling thing that's going to screw up my life for the next twenty years, and in twenty years I'll be forty-two years old, and my life will be almost over.* I felt awful, and I kind of fell apart.

> I had fantasies of harming the baby that scared me to death. I didn't want to harm her because I loved her. Of course, I told no one, because I was so ashamed and frightened. But then I decided to tell Craig, and the fantasies went away because we could talk about it.

> I didn't experience this with my second child, so it makes me think that it was, indeed, the dawning realization of the enormous responsibilities of motherhood that threw me off for those four months.

Not only do we Christian parents want our children to be well-adjusted, self-actualized, successful, contributing citizens—we also want them to grow in faith in Christ. Tricia said, "Perry and I feel a tremendous sense of responsibility for what's happening to our children. Every day I wonder if we're going to be able to make the right spiritual decisions. Are we guiding them properly?"

> **Jodi:** We let our children know that they are special not because of how they look or what they do, but because God has planned something unique for their lives.
>
> My oldest has great difficulty because of a learning disability, but I tell him that God has special plans for him, and he needs to be calm and open and try to understand what it is that should be happening in his life, so he won't miss it. I'm convinced that even his disability is going to turn into something positive in his life.
>
> Where my children are concerned, it's a challenge to keep spiritual things and emotional things in balance. I may tell them something that is spiritually true, but makes them emotionally upset. I don't want to force-feed my children with religion.
>
> I'm trying to stress *choice* as my children get older. Instead of telling them they were naughty, or that they misbehaved, I can ask them, "Do you think you made a good choice?" or "What are you going to choose to do now?"
>
> I won't always be there for my children, so they need skills for their life. They need to learn how to handle disputes with friends, to know what kinds of foods are good to eat, whatever. They need to learn how to make good choices.

Single mothers' responsibilities are multiplied. That divorced and widowed women often remarry simply to bring a second parent into the home is obvious. If mothering is lonely in its awesome responsibility, single-mothering is even more so.

Dorcas: Discipline with the children got very difficult after Harry died. Before, I could say, "You'll do this because your father and I have decided that you will." And if they didn't do it, I had back-up at the end of the day.

But when Harry died, I was in the position of being judge and jury. I had no other person to help me enforce the discipline. I felt so responsible, and I was hurting so much myself.

Audrey: I've never hated my kids, but I have hated being a mom. When I got out of my marriage, they were just one huge responsibility, and I hated that responsibility. I would come home from work, tired, and there they'd be—this gigantic mass of responsibility. Five children.

I tried to escape. I did anything I could to cope. My life was hell, even though it looked good on the outside. Mothering, for me, was not fun; it was a huge responsibility that I had to handle all by myself.

SORRY, NO GUARANTEES ISSUED

Dealing with disappointment is where the rubber meets the road when expectations and reality collide. What mother looks ahead to the time when she'll bail her daughter out of jail, drive her son to a detoxification center, or hear her child reject her most dearly held values? The disappointment when this happens is inevitable and profound.

The shame is immense, too. Good parents, good kids; bad parents, bad kids—right? I used to think so. I believed in direct cause-and-effect: if parents did a good job (cause), they'd have good children (effect). If the kids turned out bad, well . . . the proof is in the pudding, as Grandma used to say. The apple doesn't fall far from the tree, as Grandpa used to say.

The four mothers who speak next raised their children the best they could in Christian homes, yet now see that their children have gone against what they were taught.

Patricia: There are a lot of things you can do for your kids that will make a tremendous difference in their lives. On the other hand, you can go along, having done everything by the book, and then out of the blue comes some huge thing that flies in the face of all your precautions and preparations.

There's a lot I can't control in my child's life. When our first child was born, I believed that he was an empty bottle, a blank slate, and everything that George and I did would form this little person.

It's not true. Now that I've had six children, I can see that each one comes into the world with a lot of personality. They have inherent tendencies, and maybe even inherent problems.

Our son was arrested at school for drugs. He needed to be caught, to be scared and arrested for a *crime*. He needed to experience the consequences of his actions outside of what George and I would say.

I wasn't prepared for this at all. It wasn't in our job description. We didn't think that we would have to deal with a drug problem.

How did you cope?

We decided that we would be open about the problem. We could have chosen to keep it a secret, but that would have taken an enormous amount of effort. So we decided to tell people at church, friends, anybody.

And we found that there is a lot of help available: people who will support you and pray for you, counselors and youth workers. We are hooked up with one youth counseling organization that's tremendous. We'll have a problem, and tell them, "We don't know what to do about it," and they'll say, "Of course you don't. It's your first teenager, and this is the first time you've had a situation like this. So we're going to help you."

Our response was, "You mean we don't have to figure all this out for ourselves?" and they said, "No way! How could you? You have no experience." Before this, we had felt desperate, like we were the only ones with teenager problems, and we didn't know what we could or should do about it. It was a dream come true to have such support.

Most people choose to keep quiet, but I couldn't do that. I put our son on the prayer chain at church, and people came up to me and said, "Wow, I can't believe you're being so honest about this." And when he got out of the treatment center and went back to church for the first time, he said that about ten people came up to him and said that it was great to see him back and that they had been praying for him. And you know, it can be pretty scary to talk to a teenager. Intimidating. But we had been open with our church family, and they were responding with openness.

I suppose I spent a large part of my life thinking that if a kid was on drugs, the parents were screwing up. So when my own teenager got on drugs, my first reaction was probably to keep quiet about it so that I could escape other people's judgment. I know there are probably a lot of people who think that George and I *did* screw up as parents, but if you perpetuate that myth, the falsehood continues and nobody is helped. So I just had to be honest about it, and tell myself that healing was more important than discretion.

Bette: Our hyperactive child was the nearest James and I came to splitting up. He was such a problem. James didn't want to view him as a problem, but a good friend of mine absolutely insisted that we get counseling. So I went to a psychologist and when I had poured out all my feelings and desperation he said, "Why do you Christians refuse to tell yourselves about the good things you've done for this child? If he was in any other home, I'm not sure he could be in school. Why don't you get up daily and thank that God you worship that you've been able to get him this far?"

I was dumbfounded. I went home thinking, *Yeah, but I've got all these areas I haven't fixed yet.* But then I did learn to savor how far we'd come, to remember the way it used to be, to see what improvements had been made. That was a big change for me. That psychologist's challenge to believe my own God really made a difference.

I was out of control when I spanked William. He just drove me crazy, and I hated him for it. I became abusive, but I just didn't know how to stop.

So James and I talked about it, and we decided that when William needed a spanking, I would only spank three swats, and that would be it. And I would try not to do it if I was angry.

What I did was go into the bathroom and just scream my head off. I often wonder what our kids are going to think about that, the screaming.

I've talked to William about my behavior toward him. He said he doesn't remember me being out of control when I spanked him. And he says, "I'm sure I had it coming," and I reply, "I'm sure you didn't." I just didn't know how to act differently.

He's a teenager now and a really great kid. We had a very special time recently when we took a walk and I asked for his forgiveness. He put his arm around me and said, "That's okay, Mom," But there was a lot of crap—and when he gets older he's going to have to work through all that. I know that once he gets a handle on what happened, he's probably going to have to hate me for it. I don't want him to hate me, but I think I can accept that it might happen.

Janet: As the parent of a "rebellious" teenager, I felt I had to take responsibility for my son's actions. I heard this from society, from teachers—"If there's something wrong, it's the parents' fault. It's what you do at home that makes the difference." Yet I knew that we had brought up our son to believe in the Lord, to follow moral principles. Which is not to say that we were perfect parents, but I couldn't see that anything we had done would cause this sort of behavior. He was into drugs, drinking, had been caught stealing.

The Lord showed me that it's not my place to feel guilty over what my kids are doing, because God is the perfect father and even he has rebellious children. So it can't be solely the parents' responsibility; the children have an accountability of their own.

Lisa: We've had such heartaches with our children. Our son married a transsexual [a man who identifies himself as a woman] and then when his "wife" left him for another man—saying that now "she" was a lesbian—he couldn't understand what was going on. My husband and I never honored that marriage; we just didn't feel that we could, but now we have to help our son pick up the pieces.

Our other son is married to a non-Christian. And here I am, a leader in my church, a leader in the Christian community, a speaker on family life issues. I struggle with this: Should I be in a leadership role like this?

There's a lot of teaching that your children show what you're really made of, as a parent. If your kids turn out poorly, you're a poor person yourself.

When I disclose the pain and disappointment in my life, there are some who write me off as someone who doesn't deserve to be listened to. But then there are others who thank me for disclosing these personal disappointments because they feel less alone with their pain. But, boy, it's hard; I hate the criticisms. It would be so much easier just to talk about other people's problems or even about the past issues in my life that are more or less resolved at this time. But to talk about my present issues . . .

We know mothering doesn't come with a guarantee for success. If there was a foolproof formula for successful parenting, wouldn't every conscientious parent follow that formula to the letter? One mother who was getting fed-up with how-to books said, "I'm so bothered by books that say, 'If you do such and such, then your husband or children will do such and so.' It's simply not true. These are empty promises."

The mother of a university student was surprised and gratified by a conversation she had with her daughter. After a few months away at college, the young lady observed, "Mom, you know this is a really scary business, having kids. I look around and see really great parents who have really lousy kids; and I see some really good kids who have lousy parents: alcoholics, divorced, abusive. How could so many crummy kids come from such good families, and how could such good kids come from such crummy families? That's scary!"

Indeed, it is.

CHAPTER FIVE

Bread and Roses

*M*ichelle: When I got married, my hopes for romance were high. We used to spend so much time together when we were dating, talking and discussing just everything. But now, ten years later, we don't see each other very much. We don't have any time to talk.

And sex is different. I suppose I had expected—at least hoped for—the kind of sexual excitement that we used to feel for each other. But we've lost a lot of the passion. We're not unknowns to each other anymore, we're not a mystery anymore. It's really a challenge to work into a satisfying sexual relationship that isn't built on mystery and forbiddenness and . . . animal lust!

Denise: I wanted more romance than my parents had in their marriage. My father was and is practical, career-driven, a good provider. He doesn't have much inclination or time for romance. Gary, on the other hand, is very romantic, very attentive to my wants and needs, but he isn't the kind of steady provider my dad is.

Romance used to mean being married to someone who didn't put his career before me. I wanted my husband to think I was the most important thing. If I'm honest about it, I even wanted him to think I was more important than God.

When I began dating Gary, we were going to school in Texas. We took walks along the beach, we basked in the sun. It was very romantic.

On our half-year anniversary we always do something special—last year we spent the night at a nice bed-and-breakfast in a big old house. Some people would think that spending $60 on something like that—especially in our financial situation—is crazy, but it doesn't seem crazy to us.

My definition of romance has been generalized now to mean sensitivity to one another's wants and needs. We've been out with other couples, and the husband will say something careless, something that hurts his wife, but he doesn't even know it or care about it. Gary's not like that at all. He would never do anything like that. I call that romance.

You Don't Send Me Flowers Anymore

We're coming to grips with trashed hopes for great romance—that's what I heard from the women I talked to. Denise is one of only two who said their romantic expectations had been fulfilled. The other was a widow who had remarried in her seventies. She described her marriage as "total romance." Without the pressures of having to buy a house, raise children, make career decisions, and establish an adult lifestyle, this golden-years marriage is made up of shared projects, long conversations, pleasant outings, hugs and kisses, hours and hours to pray and read the Bible together. The remarried widow is my mother, and as I look at her new life with her new husband, I am eager to see the time when my impediments to romance are removed, when Steve and I can love without distraction as we did when we first met.

In the meantime, most of us are having to adjust our expectations to the reality of married life. We don't want to have to choose—romance versus practicality—but that seems to be the case.

> **Darlene:** My romantic expectations have not been realized. I thought that on Valentine's Day I'd always get flowers, that Nate would plan weekends away and do wonderful things on our anniversary. The truth is I'm lucky if he even remembers my birthday.
>
> He would never think of taking me out for a date until I mention that I feel hurt because we never go out. Then he'll do it. But I have to bring it up. He's just not a hearts-and-flowers kind of guy. Yet there's no one kinder than the man I married.
>
> His father didn't model romance. But I wish that my sons would be able to see *their* father behaving romantically toward their mother, so that they'd be able to do it when they're married. I'd like to teach them that there are some things they can do that are very nice for a woman.
>
> But if that's the worst that's wrong with my marriage, then I can't complain. I couldn't have married a kinder man.
>
> **Meredith:** Some of my romantic expectations for marriage come from my siblings. I was a teenager when my older sisters got married. One of my brothers-in-law has a reputation in our family of really liking black lace. He'll present my sister with sexy nighties and lingerie at family Christmas celebrations, with everybody there to

watch her open them up: little black shortie pajamas with red hearts on them. My other brother-in-law gives gifts of underwear and sends flowers.

Carl isn't like that. I can't picture him in a department store lingerie department picking out a present for me.

Is that okay with you?

I think gifts like that are something that any woman would appreciate. Some women are swept off their feet with flowers and candy during the courtship, and then it comes as a big shock when it stops during the marriage. It has never been a part of Carl's and my relationship. I don't know why I would have expected it, other than that I saw it in other marriages.

Paula: My father always brought us presents when he had been away on a trip, even some little cheap thing. The first time Jack went on a business trip, I expected him to bring me something. I greeted him with a gift and a card; he liked what I had done and was grateful, but it hadn't occurred to him to bring anything for me. So I cried. But now I know not to expect it.

"I Don't Suppose I'm Very Romantic Either"

The emotionally constipated, unromantic husband who makes love to his wife with the precision and creativity he applies to waxing his car has become a cultural cliché. He's the couch potato whose autumn weekends and Monday nights are devoted to football and beer; the slob who barrels into bed in boxer shorts, pocket T-shirt and nylon dress socks; the charmer who never remembers a birthday or anniversary. We see him on television sit-coms, read about him in novels, and follow his exasperating antics in the Sunday funnies.

A few women I interviewed actually claimed to be married to this man. Prejudiced as I am, this came as no surprise. What *did* surprise me was to hear several women admit that *they* were willing to take responsibility for lack of romance in their marriages.

> **Robin:** I believe that my parents killed my appreciation for beauty. It wasn't valued by them, and I lost my value for it. Consequently, I didn't know how to respond to my husband's romantic behavior.
>
> He wrote me poetry, he talked to me about his deepest thoughts and feelings. And I had to be trained to respond to this. When I didn't respond, he backed off because it wasn't being rewarded. Now, we've met each other halfway.
>
> I know it's my fault that there isn't more romance in our relationship now.

> **Melissa:** After my husband has been on the road, traveling, he wants three things to be there when he gets home: Coke, ice, and white bread. Our biggest fight came after he had returned from several trips in a row and those things weren't there for him—because I don't use them if he's not around.
>
> When he works in town, he expects me to fix him a lunch. Not that the maid will fix him a lunch, but that I will do it. If I don't provide these things, it comes across to him as though I don't care about him.

While some women are mourning the loss of romance—regardless of who is at fault—others are arriving at a different understanding of the place of romance in marriage. How does it interact with commitment or with security issues?

Denise: My husband cooks dinner every night, after his long day at work; he makes my lunch for me; he does the laundry; he takes me out to movies and dinner; he remembers every little thing I like. At Christmas he showers me with gifts, picking up on things I've said throughout the year, giving me exactly what I would like. He's absolutely thoughtful, attentive to my needs.

I know there are husbands who forget their wife's birthday, who don't help around the house. But maybe they are hardworking at their jobs, and maybe they take their financial responsibilities seriously. Maybe they don't call when they're away on a business trip, but at least they have the kind of job that's responsible and important enough that they even *take* a business trip. These are the things that are putting a strain on our marriage.

My grandmother and grandfather probably had no love in their marriage, but for fifty years my grandfather brought home a paycheck and supported his family. Is that love?

Karen: I thought that things would be a little more romantic, like *The Gift of the Magi* by O. Henry. Bob is not romantic, he just isn't. I'm not sure I know any men who are, but I had read enough Russian novels and romances to wish that Bob would be.

He has become more sensitive to this wish; he makes an effort to do the little things that will make me feel loved: a note on my windshield that he leaves as he goes to work, a remembered anniversary of when we started dating, that sort of thing.

When we were first married, I wanted him to know what I liked and disliked, but I wanted it to be something intuitive, something that he just knew. Then I realized that if he was to know these things about me, I was going to have to give him some help. I would have to tell him or make it possible for him to discover it himself.

Such as?

One of my first Mother's Day presents came from the hardware store, which is not where I think those kinds of gifts should come from. Later there happened to be a cartoon in the paper about a man who had given his wife a washing machine for Mother's Day. I cut that out and said to Bob, "There are some really great things that come from the hardware store, but what I would like more is a nightgown or something like that. Perfume, something a little more personal." He was willing to hear what I had to say. Now, we even joke about it. When it's my birthday or something, he'll say, "Well, I'm off to the hardware store. . . ."

I have a friend who gets flowers and candy and love notes from her husband all the time. But that's all she gets. He won't fix a faucet or shovel the snow. When it gets right down to it, I know that Bob loves me because he's the one who gets up with the children at night, and he works around the house, and he's available for me and the kids. And in the end, that means a lot more than daisies on the breakfast table.

Suzanne: I haven't given up all my romantic notions—I still would like my husband to send me flowers, and surprise me with little thoughtful acts. But I have given up, most definitely, *the* romantic notion of a man who will take care of me.

Happiness comes only in moments—and I think that's enough! I don't think you can live your life in a state of perpetual bliss; that's not what life is all about. It's not real. The romantic notion is fine when it happens, but I don't believe it makes for lasting relationships. Marriage is day-to-day, every day. That's what a lasting relationship is—commitment, in spite of all the hassles.

"NOT ALWAYS GREAT"

Marriage counselors say that when a couple's sex life is good, they tend to think sex isn't a big part of their relationship. But when sex is bad, they consider it the most crucial component. Many of the women I asked about their sex lives gave short answers: "It's okay . . . we're doing fine . . . no problems." Some of them, I'm sure, just weren't going to talk to me about it; others were content and didn't have much to say—that is, sex was good.

I can relate. Steve and I were once asked by a friend (we wouldn't do it for a stranger!) to be interviewed on Valentine's Day by his college class on Marriage and Family. It was the holiday aspect that kept me from realizing what we were getting into, I suppose.

So there we were, the Lawheads and another couple, at the front of a lecture hall facing a couple hundred university students. After fifteen minutes of easy questions they got down to why we were all there.

"How's sex?" asked a young undergrad. Everyone in the hall leaned forward in their chairs. Except me. I slouched back in mine.

Luckily, the other wife answered first. "Not always great," she replied.

"Ditto," I said. And we went on to elaborate for the remainder of the hour.

Several women I talked to were, unlike me, eager to talk about past and present difficulties.

Marjorie: I had a friend who was non-orgasmic. She lived in a really little town out West; there wasn't much help for her there. So she decided that she would go to some of the older women in her church and see what help they could give her. Can you imagine what happened? One of them said, "I don't know what that word means."

I was non-orgasmic, and that was a big disappointment. Scripturally, we're told to enjoy sex. I remember reading 1 Corinthians, where Paul said the only reason not to have sex is for prayer—I laughed! I hated sex.

We went to Masters and Johnson, read a lot, got a lot of help. I felt very alone in this, as though we had to find out everything for ourselves. Maybe everybody feels this way, I don't know. But I do think that there is a lack of information. It's not that women don't know where the penis goes; it's that they don't know anything about their own sexuality, their own sexual makeup. That needs to be developed between a husband and wife.

Most women are being rushed into intercourse. They need more time to get aroused. You ask a woman, any woman, when she was most aroused in her life and it was probably when she was dating, when she was necking and petting in the backseat of her boyfriend's car. She felt secure, she felt loved. The taboos forced her boyfriend to spend lots of time with her in what is really foreplay. That has to happen in marriage, too.

Nicolette: I was very naive sexually when I got married. Our honeymoon was a nightmare. "It" wasn't working. We had to go to a doctor—on our honeymoon—to see why we couldn't manage intercourse. I was scared, I was small. He was anxious, he was big. A basic incompatibility!

I wanted sex to be something wonderful, and it turned out to be a crock. It didn't quit *hurting* until after our first child was born. It sure wasn't fulfilling. I was on the pill, and my libido was crap on the pill. I had no knowledge that being on the pill is like being semi-pregnant, in terms of hormones, and that being pregnant often brings a decrease in sexual interest. Nobody told me. I thought it was all *me*. I thought something was wrong with *me*.

I was a pretty reserved person. My personality was flat. Well, I just wasn't horny. I didn't get aroused. I *was* orgasmic once I got to the proper stage, but I was never aroused before the encounter, and that seemed like it would be so much fun!

It was the disappointment of my life. My hope was that I would be as interested in sex as Dave was, that our appetites would be the same, and—bottom-line—that vaginal intercourse would be as satisfying as clitoral stimulation.

I was so naive! I thought the penis would go through the clitoris! When I found out it didn't, I thought God had made a terrible mistake. He'd done it all wrong. I still think it might have been engineered differently; I plan on asking him about it someday.

There were other things, too. Like mutual orgasm. I thought this would come easily. It took fifteen years to achieve *a* mutual orgasm, and even at that I'm starting to think we lucked out.

Our sexual dynamic has always been volatile—we'll be doing okay for a while, and then we'll crash and true feelings will come out:

"I don't like this."

"Oh, yeah, well, I don't like it either. And another thing . . ."

"I want more!"

"You always want more!"

"So divorce me!"

"I can't divorce you because I love you. And if we never had sex again I'd still love you . . ."

"Oh, okay. Let's go on."

All the time, I'd be thinking *I've got to get better, I've got to get better.* But there was no "better" to get; I was really stuck.

Ruth: I think sex is very frustrating. I'm always very tired, I've been pawed on all day by the children, I don't want to have sex at the end of the day. My poor husband . . . he's so denied.

Before I figured out that lots of women are tired, I wondered what was wrong with me, why I wasn't turned on for my husband all the time. But I've talked to a lot of mothers about this, and most of them are saying the same thing: they're not interested in sex.

I told Jim about this, and he said, "Fine, but that doesn't make it right. It just helps explain it some."

I suppose it's motherhood, because if I'm not pregnant, I'm nursing. And maybe it's a hormonal thing. But I don't want sex. And that's a little disappointing because when we were first married, we had sex all the time and it was really fun. But now, I guess I'd rather have a backrub than make love!

How are you dealing with this?

I pray about it. I sure don't like to read about it. Books about sex make me sick. I don't like to read, "And then you put your hand . . ."

When we were first married, I was mushy all the time. And then it mellowed out a little. Then I had children, and my energies went toward them. My love for my husband is different, less childish. Deeper. Maybe that's the way it should be, I don't know. Sometimes I feel guilty about it.

Do you remember what they used to say when we just got married? If you put a penny in a jar each time you made love during the first year of marriage, and then took a penny out each time you made love for the rest of your married life, you'd still have pennies in the jar when you died.

I didn't believe that when I got married. I couldn't imagine that it wouldn't always be just wonderful to make love, that we wouldn't do it all the time. But there's a lot of truth in that penny illustration. Do you remember in "Fiddler on the Roof," where Tevye asks Golda, "Do you love me?" I think it would be better if we would live by our commitment, not our words—and not by how often we have sex.

The Total Woman makes me barf. Wrapping up in Saran Wrap, making love underneath the dining room table. I hate that. In Mary Pride's book *The Way Home* she has a chapter about "unkinky sex." I thought, right on! We're not *supposed* to be constantly turned on, making sexual experimentation and variations the focus of our physical relationships with our husbands. Mary Pride doesn't think you're a total write-off as a woman if you don't wear teddies and garter belts around the house, that you're depriving your husband of something he has a right to. I thought that was really neat—that married sex is something more than the gunky stuff you see on billboards. I can't go along with these other books, where they're trying to tell you how to be a sexual athlete.

I don't want to be turned on. I don't mind satisfying my husband, but I just don't want to be turned on. But there are all kinds of people who are telling me that isn't okay; I've got to *want* sex. I don't think so. My sexual relationship isn't anything less. The Bible doesn't say you have to be turned on all the time; it just says to give yourself to your husband.

WORKING IT OUT

In our society, in these times of high quality everything, a poor sex life is unacceptable; an "okay" sex life is one that needs work; an exciting sex life is demanded: great frequency, simultaneous and multiple orgasms, innovation and stamina. How are women coping with these standards for performance?

Suzanne: Right now, my husband's expectations for a sexual relationship are suffering—I'm tired a lot!

I expend a tremendous amount of energy elsewhere. Sex takes a lot of energy—at least working up to it takes a lot of energy; once you're into it, it doesn't seem like energy is any question. I always have plenty at that point.

I think this is a problem between Tom and me: he can't ever get affection and sex figured out. I could use more affection—kisses and hand-holding and hugs and all that. He could use more sex; he thinks sex is affection.

117

My husband is very straightforward and inventive, sexually. He's got great imagination. Physically, he's a wonderful mate for me—his size fits my size. And he knows what I like. Put me in with the "satisfied women."

Melissa: We're slipping into the routine of the Sunday afternoon snuggle, every-other-night sex. It's pretty much a turn-out-the-lights-and-get-under-the-covers affair. It's a routine. Neither one of us is concerned about performance or variety.

It's predictable. And I don't think either one of us is dissatisfied, although I am beginning to think that I could spice things up a little bit now and then, as a preventive measure, perhaps. After all, Frank travels with women he works with (which was a little hard for me to get used to at first), and he works with attractive, stylish women who are his equal, professionally. We've seen a lot of marriages fall apart under these circumstances. So I look at that with a little nervousness. I'm beginning to think I'd better keep on my toes, make sure I don't turn into a boring slob.

So I could get a little more adventurous—not out of fear, but out of a realistic belief that an ounce of prevention is worth a pound of cure. I could make the first move more often. I could send the kids out to play and seduce him when he comes home from work. Those are things I don't do now—because they aren't convenient. But I could.

Emily: Sex is better as we get closer. And it's really a treat once you've had kids—*if* you ever get a chance to do it.

Wendy: I think most people—myself included—go into marriage thinking that you have to make love with a certain frequency or things aren't right. I used to get really panicky about that. I would cry, and think, *I'm terrible, what's wrong with me.* . . .

I wish I could tell people who are at that place now, "Just be patient. Don't worry." It only gets better if you can relax and quit worrying about how many times a week or month you make love. There are bound to be times when it's very difficult to find any opportunities—when you're pregnant, maybe, when you have babies who are getting up at night, when you're sick. Just try to work through those times. It won't last forever, and it will get better.

To Know, and Be Known

Rose: I have always wanted to know and be known. It isn't happening in my marriage; I'm resigned to this reality: I won't be known in the way I want this side of heaven.

I do think Paul and I have come to have greater understanding; he is a much more understanding person now than he was when we got married, and in that way I think I've been a blessing to him. And he's been a blessing to me, too. He has initiated a lot of confrontations with reality in our relationship, and I see that as growth. He's forced me to deal with the difference between what I want and what I get.

My expectation was that the primary goal of our family life would be understanding, intimacy.

Intimacy has to do with trust, with communication, with sharing the very deepest secrets, with knowing another person, and being known. Some relationships grow into intimacy, others don't. "My husband is like a houseguest," lamented **Florence**.

"He's polite, and he'll help out if I ask him to. But that's where it stops." She continues:

> My husband doesn't seem to want intimacy. I've talked to a friend about this, and she feels the same way about her husband. And from the latest Hite Report, it sounds like this is par for the course. My husband doesn't want to say to me, "This is what's going on with me, this is how I feel about what happened to me this week."

> He'll tell me *what* happened, but he doesn't want to get into how he *feels* about it. He doesn't ask me how I feel, he doesn't seem to notice what's going on in my life. Mark can talk intellectually, or he can talk about practical matters, but not about feelings.

> I can force Mark to talk to me. I can insist that he sit down with me, and I can tell him I need to talk, and he'll say, "Okay, then, what do you want to talk about?" and I'll start sharing or asking questions and he's got this look on his face that means what he's really thinking is, *I wonder if my game is still on TV?* or *When will this be over?* He looks like he's in pain. And these aren't threatening conversations! I could be saying wonderful things about him and what he does and our children . . . but he can't stand it.

> My friend wants more intimacy, too. But her husband doesn't want it; he's perfectly satisfied with the way things are between them. She thinks it's intolerable.

> This is surely why people have affairs. They meet someone who is suddenly interested in them, interested in what they wear and what they do and what they say and what they *feel.* If there isn't that sort of interest at home, it starts looking pretty good when it's offered from the outside.

Jeanine: If I can't trust Roger to be home on time for dinner, how can I trust him with the deepest secrets of my heart?

Meredith: If I cry, he walks out of the room. Carl won't have anything to do with me when I'm sad like this. I've told him it's real hard for me when he does this, but he can't or won't deal with this kind of sadness.

He was very supportive of me during the funeral after my sister died. But as soon as we got back to our own home he expected the grief to be over. But it wasn't—it isn't—for me.

This is the area where our expectations differ most. On an intellectual level I can say, "We're from different backgrounds, this is just his way, it doesn't have anything to do with his love for me," but on an emotional level I still want him to relate to me in ways that I can understand.

Katherine: One crisis point occurred early in our marriage. Stan was doing a bit of traveling, and I asked him if he missed me when he was gone. We had already set a pattern of honesty, so he said, "No,"—he didn't miss me when he was gone. So then I said, "Let me see if I hear what you're saying. I hear you say that when you are traveling and we're apart, you don't miss me."

We knew how to talk; we know how to not be defensive; we knew how to make "I" statements instead of "you" statements. And we did it well; but when we got down to the practical nitty-gritty of it, I was left with this: my husband travels and is away, and when he's away, he doesn't miss me.

We stayed up almost all night, with me saying things like, "Have I got this straight? Did you just say that you don't miss me?" and him trying to find less emotional and more kind ways of honestly saying, "No, I don't." He didn't miss me. But he was my *life* at that time. There was nothing else.

Virginia: I did hope that there would be deeper communication. I thought that we would talk about everything, in depth—and that we would communicate intimately.

I remember someone telling me that in a restaurant you can always tell who's married; they are the ones who are not talking, just eating. And I thought, *That won't be true of us. We'll always have a lot to talk about.* But I was wrong. We don't have a lot to talk about. Maybe we do have a lot to talk about, but we don't do it. That's a disappointment.

HOW CLOSE CAN WE GET?

Hearing all this has caused me to give thought to the level of intimacy I enjoy with Steve. I've always thought we were intimate on every level: physically, emotionally, spiritually. I do know that when we're in a restaurant, we're talking to each other. In fact, we've always thought that the silent couples were the ones who didn't have children at home interrupting every conversation and forcing their parents to eat at restaurants just so they can decide what color to paint the bathroom ceiling.

But having raised the issue, I really can't stop thinking about it. Am I sharing with him on the deepest level I can? I really have no way of knowing how deeply he's sharing with me—he might be holding back a great deal. Who knows?

When Florence talked about the Hite Report—this latest, third installment—I remembered that the Hite

Report indicated that many women are turning to other women for the intimacy lacking in their marriages. How sad this is, but certainly it's true: I have women friends I can talk to about things I can't talk to Steve about.

Theresa is the minister of a congregation in northern California and has made this observation about the women in her parish:

> I have a theory that most women are single. They may be married, but inside they're single. And they're more role-playing than living.
>
> Most of their relationships are with women, most of their meaningful communication is with women. They had expected that their intimacy would be with their husbands, but finding this impossible, they seek it with other women outside their marriages. They've had to leave their families, emotionally, in order to have their needs met.
>
> People get married for the wrong reasons. The ten most common reasons for getting married have nothing to do with relationship. They're such things as sex, marrying to forget a broken relationship, to have children, to get out of the house, out of the belief that nobody else will every marry me so I'd better marry this person who will. None of these reasons has to do with relationship.
>
> I'm finding that most married people don't have true companionship—they lead parallel lives, not lives that intersect. And young people realize this; I talk to teenagers and women in their early twenties who see no good reason for being married because they don't see happy, fulfilled, intimate married people.

THE INFIDELITIES OF MARRIAGE

A Christian speaker I know begins her marriage workshops for men by asking a question: "What are you going to do *when* you fall in love with another woman?" It's a question of when, not if. And it's just as true for women—if we haven't had it happen already, it will soon enough: we'll be seriously attracted to another man, and we'll have to decide what we're going to do. How will we handle the temptations to have an affair, to leave our husbands, to change our convictions to suit our emotions?

Anna: When I married Phillip, I thought he was just great. I knew that he was the person I wanted to spend my whole life with. I knew everything wouldn't be rosy, but he was the person I wanted to stick it out with. It felt right. He was a Christian, so I knew that spiritually we were going to make it. We had a lot of interests in common. I expected that we would stay together.

The first four years of marriage were total hell. Are we talking about marriage? Total hell. Most people go through something awful, but they say, "I'd do it again." Even with our kids and even though things are okay now, I can't say I'd do it again.

What was going on?

My husband didn't want to be married to me. He didn't want to get married the day of our wedding, and I knew that. He wanted to be independent, he wanted to be with his friends more—but we went ahead with the wedding because it was all planned.

We were both in graduate school. For Phillip, school and his friends—men friends and *women* friends—were his whole life. There was nothing left for me. He wasn't in the marriage.

And I was dying. I felt rejected, unwanted, unloved. I lost all confidence in who I was as a person and what I could do. I was nervous. I could hardly talk to people. I was stuttering. It makes me nauseous to remember all this.

It took him four years to decide that he wanted to be married.

What changed?

He decided that it was okay to be married. But by then, I was sort of on my way out. He had told me not to rely on him, to get some other friends. So I got some friends. I met another man, and he wanted to marry me.

So I went to Phillip and said, "What are we going to do about this? He's getting serious about our relationship, and I'm on my way out of this marriage."

I wanted to be married to Phillip, but I couldn't do it by myself. I didn't want to get divorced, and I didn't want to be involved with someone else. But I was absolutely and completely desperate. The events of my life were going against everything I believed in. At the time, we were living in a Christian commune! I kept thinking about the Bible and what it said about relationships, and marriage, and all that.

But I couldn't take any more rejection. I couldn't take any more torture. I was almost dead as a person, emotionally dead.

Then one day he decided that it was okay to be married, okay for him to be married to me. (This is how he would say it if he were here.) We knew we had to answer some questions about commitment, and what we wanted and how we were going to get it. We did move out of the commune, because it wasn't working anymore.

I let him know that it was him I wanted to be married to, that he was the one I loved. Everything else was done out of desperation. We started getting our act together. We decided we did want to stay together.

What was it like after that?

It was a relief. But I haven't forgotten what happened. Even now, years later, I live in fear that someday he'll decide that he doesn't want to be married to me, and there won't be anything I can do about it if he makes that decision.

Maybe I'll be smarter if it happens again. I'll see it coming before it's too late. I'll be more aggressive if I think that he's distancing himself from our relationship. I'll have that history, I'll be able to say, "Is this like last time? Are we moving in that direction?"

Anita: I've read that marital infidelity—on the man's part—is highest during the wife's pregnancy and after the birth of children. It's easy to see why that is. It was hard enough for me to give up intercourse, and I can imagine it's even harder for a husband because he doesn't have the experiences of pregnancy, childbirth, and the tactile contact of nursing to counterbalance the abstinence.

Recently the possibility of having an affair with a married man—a Christian—presented itself. Although many things were strong in my marriage, there was not a real cherishing of each other. After so many years of marriage and so many children, maybe we were taking each other for granted. And here comes someone who opens my doors, and treats me with respect, and understands a lot about me.

You were tempted.

I suppose I was. And I could have done two things: I could have kept my temptation secret, or I could have shared the whole thing with Chuck. I chose to tell my husband. And things really changed for us. We started spending more time together; we spent hours in the bedroom, talking; we started behaving differently toward one another. On one occasion, I sang to my husband—I've never done anything like that before. Another time, we were making love, and Chuck started praying, right at the end. That was a first, too—very out of character, really.

So this is a happy ending?

We came out of it with an appreciation for our relationship we hadn't had before. We realized that to lose what we have would be totally devastating. We would be destroyed.

I once said to Chuck, "If you ever have an affair, that will be the end of our family." I thought he had to know that on the night that he chose to have sex with another woman, that would be it for us. I would take the kids and he would have nothing.

I felt he needed a strong motivation to be faithful. I wanted him to know that when he was out of town for a convention, and he went to the hotel bar after a meeting, and a willing woman sat next to him at the bar, and he contemplated what he was going to do . . . to have sex that night would mean the end of our marriage and estrangement from his kids. I felt he needed a voice saying, "It will cost you everything if you do it."

You're talking in the past tense.

Because I'm not so sure about it anymore. I ask myself, "Would you really do it? Would you take the children and leave for that offense, that breach of trust?" And I can't say for certain that I would.

Marjorie: My husband was involved with another woman. It went on for a few years—he was in way over his head. We talked about it, I confronted him on it and told him that he had to make a decision—it was going to be either her or me. He couldn't have both. So he broke off the relationship, but subsequently I found that he was still involved with her. He was writing to her, he was still attached to her.

It was a very difficult time for us; there was a lot of anger and hurt. But it didn't break up our marriage. We weren't going to let it do that. In the end, I think our marriage is actually stronger for it (although I can't recommend it to other couples who have marriage difficulties!).

God helped me to allow Warren to have time to work on that. He felt that this woman was the only woman besides me who had ever expressed an interest in him sexually, who thought he was desirable. Men seem to have this need the same as women do—the need to be thought desirable.

I had to learn that I was not responsible for Warren's choice. It was not a fault in me that drew him to her. But we're taught, as women, that we can hang onto our men if we have sex with them enough, flatter them enough, do whatever they need. It's our responsibility.

But I learned that it all had nothing to do with me; it was Warren's decision. Similarly, I can't excuse myself by saying, "Warren doesn't have sex with me enough, Warren doesn't listen to me when I talk, Warren doesn't attend to me emotionally . . . I deserve an affair." It's no good to say, "If only." "If only he were someone

different, if only he would do this, if only he
would understand that." It gets you nowhere.

THE IMPOSSIBLE POSSIBILITY

Is it too much to expect that our husbands will be
romantic, good providers, sensitive sexual partners
who never pressure us? That they will share their deepest secrets and want to know our own? That they will
remain faithful and true? Would we be happy, then, if
they would do all these things for us?

Hazel: I was taught, as a child, that if I
followed the Lord with all my heart, the Bible
meant just exactly what it said: that you can't
outgive the Lord, but that there would be sacrifice. There would be sacrifice, and persecution—
but also tremendous blessing that would com-
pensate for the hardships.

I expected to live with the man I married, and
as it turned out, that's where the sacrifice came
in. We were missionaries in China, and my husband traveled in the outlying villages two to three
weeks a month. I was young, in a foreign country, and very alone. I've spent 50 or 60 percent of
my married life alone, and I didn't count on that.
It was a grinding sacrifice that I had to cope with
every day. And the only way I could accept it was
to realize the sovereignty of God, and to know
that he was allowing it to happen.

I have to be careful to not expect Lawrence
to do for me what only God can do. Lawrence
can't fulfill me, but God can. I had to learn this.
When I expected Lawrence to do something that
was God's business, I became unhappy with him
and frustrated. I realized I was looking to
Lawrence for everything, and when that happens,
it kills a man. He becomes stifled, too. It made

him miserable because I was clinging to him, wanting to hold him back.

Bette: James was supposed to make me happy. Well, he never hit the mark. And I got easily discouraged with our marriage because while we were dating I was his whole life. And once we got married, he had his schooling, his job . . . I was about third fiddle, I thought. The first five or six years weren't too bad, but always there was this expectation that he should make me happy.

I think that all women, but Christian women in particular, have to come to the point where they grapple with this question of who their God is. Is it their husband? We say our husbands come after God, but I think we only *say* that. Practically speaking, we look to our husbands for our happiness and our life.

What is it like to be responsible for another person's happiness, another person's life? Pregnant women and mothers of infants know the feeling of being indispensable for a season; gradually, though, they learn to adjust their lives and their relationship with their child as years of absolute dependence pass by and the child becomes a self-sufficient individual.

But what would it be like to be a man married to a woman who is depending on you for every material, spiritual, emotional and social happiness—a woman who will not grow out of that need?

Is this a man's God-given responsibility? Is that what it means for the husband to be head of the wife? Is it what our churches are encouraging in the "biblical" marriage?

Before we move on to issues relating to personal growth, listen carefully to Ellen as she struggles to grow within the context of the marriage she has with Raoul.

ELLEN'S STORY

At the age of thirty, Ellen expected to be a stay-at-home mother, married to a man who is progressing in a stable career, living in her own home. Yet her husband's job is not secure; she herself is ambivalent about a promotion being presented at work; and as a couple Ellen and Raoul are wondering what to do about their infertility. Their one pregnancy ended in miscarriage.

Several of my expectations haven't been fulfilled. I assumed we'd be more established by this time: that Raoul would be out of school, that we'd have children and I'd be able to stay home with those children, that Raoul's career would be going somewhere, that we'd have a house or at least a nicer place to live.

For the first four years of marriage, all that was okay. But suddenly, it wasn't okay any more. I knew that things would be hard when we got married. He wasn't done with school, we didn't have money. But I didn't think it would last this long.

I'm not your typical career woman. I never wanted to be. I hate to admit it, but I went to a Christian college to . . .to find a husband and get married. I thought that the little dream I had—of a home, children, homemaking—was okay. It was traditional, it was biblical, no problems. And I didn't have to have it immediately, it just had to be on the horizon.

Now I realize I may have to give up that dream altogether. It hasn't happened yet, and it may never happen. I have to find a way to be happy and content and fulfilled.

STRUGGLING WITH INFERTILITY

Infertility hasn't been good for our sex life. When we were first married, we tried different kinds of birth control but nothing was very satisfactory, so we just quit using it because we wanted to have children eventually, and we wouldn't mind having them sooner rather than later. But then I didn't get pregnant and I didn't get pregnant.

I began to lose interest in sex because it wasn't accomplishing what it was supposed to. I quit thinking of it as something that was pleasurable for its own sake, and started thinking of it as something that was supposed to produce a child, but *didn't*.

Every month, when it was time for my period, I'd wonder if I'd be pregnant. And month after month I'd have my period, which meant I wasn't pregnant. It was such a tense time, waiting to find out if I was or wasn't.

If you don't have sex the tension is gone because you *know* you aren't going to be pregnant. So I didn't want to have sex because it was unproductive, and the fact that it *could* be productive made me tense.

At the same time, I was becoming dissatisfied in my marriage, and blaming it on Raoul which made it easy to find fault with him: he's irresponsible, he's not spiritual enough, he's overweight, on and on. That compounded the sex problem, because I couldn't be sexually attracted to someone with so many faults.

What's the solution?

Things have gotten better only since I started counseling, because I have been able to identify these components and get some help in devising strategies to deal with them.

Is it really that I don't love Raoul any more, that I find him unattractive? No.

I've been trying to go back to doing the things that used to be pleasurable, romantic. I used to pick up Raoul from work late at night. I'd put on a negligee and then just my coat over that and pick him up from work. And when we got home there would be candles lit in the bedroom, a really nice romantic atmosphere for love-making.

Well, I hadn't done anything like that for a long, long time. But I started to do it again. I tried to think in romantic terms, tried to think about all the positive things about Raoul that I loved. And I tried to remember sex as a pleasurable thing we shared, not a procreative act.

Since I don't have children, I'd like to be the kind of wife who is really sexy, really attractive to her husband, available to him physically. I guess those are things that are harder when you're pregnant, or nursing, or taking care of little kids.

I probably can't have children, biologically, but I could still adopt children. Raoul and I have been working with a children's home, and we're investigating the possibility of adopting. I know that being a family is more than giving birth to babies; it's living in love with children—raising children to know God and have a relationship with him.

I thought I'd conceive and be able to be pregnant, which seems like the most wonderful thing in the world to me. We'd have a little boy or a little girl who would look like Raoul or like me, or like both of us.

Now . . . we've been talking about transracial adoption because that's probably our best chance for getting a child. This little boy or little girl isn't going to look anything like Raoul or me. And we'll have the job of teaching that child that it's okay to be different, of integrating that child into its ethnic culture and acquainting it with its racial heritage. Well, I didn't anticipate this. I thought the child would participate in *my* culture.

And there are other parts of the dream that die, too. Will Raoul ever have a job that makes enough money and is steady enough so that I can afford to stay home with a child? Or will I have to drop him or her off at a day-care center while I go to work? And then when we all get home will we have any energy left for any kind of family life? Because if it's going to be a big rush all the time, and a dirty house, and no strength to do anything fun, and substituting "quality time" for the needed quantity of time—I'm not sure I want that either.

My dream of family life came, in part, from my childhood. My mother reminds me that I always wanted to be a housewife when I was a little girl. And then I have gone to some very conservative churches, where the ideal is for a woman to be married and have children and stay home and care for those children. I agree with this. I think that it's probably right to say that a woman's greatest and primary role is as a wife and mother.

Last week I was asked, "Is this really biblical, or are you turning it into something biblical?" The question is, is my wish for a home and family something that I want so desperately that I'm using the Bible to validate it?

I need to spend some time reading and thinking and praying. Perhaps the idea that women should be at home isn't biblical. Right now, I believe it is. Maybe if I get a different perspective it will help me accept my infertility and my marriage as it is, not as I wish it was.

"I Don't Fit In"

I don't fit in with women who are totally career-minded. They don't seem to care if they ever get married; if they are married, they have no interest in having children.

I don't feel I fit in with the women at church. Most of them are stay-at-home mothers. When they get together they love to talk about their kids. I can understand that, but if you want kids desperately and know you can't have them, then it's pretty hard to take. I feel like crying when I get in those situations.

If one more person talks to me about the Proverbs 31 woman . . . gosh, I just hate her! When you talk about women's roles, it seems that everyone comes back to the Proverbs 31 woman! There's so little in the Bible about women's roles . . . about being a wife and a mother. I wish there were more.

I don't know what it means when it says that wives should submit to their husbands. I don't know what it means when it says that husbands should exercise leadership in their families.

I thought my husband would be the spiritual leader in our marriage. The problem is that Raoul was a new Christian when we got married, he came from a non-Christian home; he had no background for "spiritual leadership." I've been a Christian for many years, I come from a Christian home; I grew up in the church; I have a greater interest in spiritual things. I like to discuss spiritual and theological issues, I like to think about things that never cross Raoul's mind.

Raoul was asked to pray aloud in church a few Sundays ago, and I almost broke into a sweat. I knew he'd never done it before and that he wouldn't know what to say. I know he'll never be asked to teach Sunday school because he simply doesn't know enough to teach. My friends' husbands teach Sunday school, and they lead worship, or even preach—but my husband won't do that, probably never. And I'm tired of being ashamed of that, and I'm tired of always wishing that it would be different.

I don't have answers on this. But I know that I'm not willing to say that because I'm more educated than he is, and I'm more motivated, and I've been a Christian longer, and I'm more vocal and outgoing that I'm willing to take on the leadership role in our marriage. I still think that it's supposed to rest with him. But I don't know how that's going to happen.

He would let me take control. I don't want that to happen. But I don't want to be ashamed of who he is, either.

I'm trying to think about the future. I'm trying to work on my dreams. I'm trying to decide how I feel about having a career. My boss is leaving; I could have her job.

I'm doing a lot of reading on adoption, trying to accept the idea of raising children who are not my own biologically.

I'm trying to get some answers to my questions about submission, spiritual leadership, and my role. I'm trying to accept Raoul right now, as he is, and yet still look forward to a future where he will have grown.

An update: Raoul has received a good promotion at work, and Ellen took over her boss's job. No children yet.

CHAPTER SIX

Personal Growth

One child is learning to keep quiet during kindergarten story time; his classmate is learning to speak up when she has a question. A mother of four is learning to set standards in the home, and consequently, how to discipline; her best friend is learning how to let children exercise their independence. Husband A is learning to say "I love you" to his wife; Husband B is learning to *show* his wife that he loves her instead of just talking about it all the time. I am learning to be more easy-going; you may be learning to be more assertive.

We are all learning different skills, different concepts; we each have our growing edge. Yet we hope, in the end, to arrive at the same place: a point of balance, of consistency and truth.

LEARNING TO BE STRONG

We may not know if we can stand alone until we are forced, by circumstances, to do just that. Surrounded by people, institutions, and material props that provide support, it may take a crisis to force the question: can we be strong, can we survive?

Three women below found what strength they had when family support was taken away—by divorce, by death, and by rejection.

Phyllis: I got married when I was twenty, waited a few years to have children, and then stayed home raising my three kids. My husband had the job, I did volunteer work in the church.

After a time, I went to college. I took all the classes in the evening so it wouldn't disrupt my home responsibilities, made arrangements for the babysitter, did it all. I took two courses at a time; it took me ten years to get a bachelor's degree.

When my youngest child was in kindergarten, I got a job teaching school. It was all working pretty well until I was thirty-nine. I'd been married nineteen years, and I started to change.

It was a mid-life reevaluation. I started to reevaluate my relationships with men, my relationship with the church, with my family . . . everything. That was ten years ago, and for ten years I've been in transition.

All my coping mechanisms, all my values, everything that my family and society had given me, disintegrated. They didn't work. They left me with confusion, doubt, and conflict in every area of my life: conflicts religiously, conflicts as a mother, conflicts as a wife, conflicts as an in-law, conflicts as a daughter. I began a search at that time that has only been resolved in the last few months.

I left the church I was raised in, I left my teaching job, and went out into ministry. A few weeks ago, I finally left my marriage.

It was a spiritual crisis and an identity crisis that started all this in motion. Much of it had to do with a crisis that centers around my identity as a woman.

As a woman, I feel I should have freedom. I should not be connected to any other person for my identity. I should be free to choose and decide how to spend my day, where I will go and what I will do. I should be viewed by others as a valuable and credible person. I should be listened to.

I've been told that I come on too strong, I have too many opinions. My husband, ever since I first met him, has said, "No one can handle you." Well, why do I have to be "handled"? Does he have to be handled? Am I such a threat? Is it because I'm educated? Why does my education equip me to be at home, making everything right at home, while the same education given to a man equips him to solve problems in the business world, or to participate in a church ministry?

I should be able to contribute without the aggression that males have. Without their anger. And I don't think I should have to receive it, either.

Dorcas: Before I was married the first time, I had boyfriends. When Harry died and I was single again, I thought that there would be nice men around and that I would probably get married again. But then I realized that, no, there aren't a lot of nice men around. They're all married now. And if they aren't married, they soon will be because there are a lot of single women for every single man.

When one relationship failed after about a year, I made up my mind that I would not marry again because the type of man I wanted simply wasn't available. I decided that I would try to become a complete person on my own.

I had to do a lot of growing. I had had a good marriage, and when Harry died it was like having an amputation. There was a raw edge, an open part to me that had to heal and had to grow. Eventually, I think I did heal, but it took much longer than I thought.

People expected me to be "over it," to quit grieving Harry's death, and to get my life in order. I was lonely because I felt that I couldn't admit to still being in this process. You don't get over your husband's death in a year or so.

There's that continuing, nagging loneliness and confusion and pain. I used to wonder if my heart would ever sing again. Could I ever be exuberant about anything?

I think you became a better person after Harry died.

I had so much to learn, so much business to take care of. I had to find a job. I went back to school, and after that I was accepted into graduate school. And I got a better job. I had to be a better person in order to survive, to earn a living and support my family. I had to make decisions— sell one house and buy another, and then another after that. I had to decide on repairs, furniture, cars. I balanced my own checkbook. These were things I had never done before.

It was all new to me. I had to learn. And you can't learn without improving.

When I was accepted to graduate school, I felt like skipping down the hall. I was fifty-five years old, and I was in graduate school! And then when I got a job—that was just a miracle. I met people who didn't know whose wife I had been, or whose daughter. It was rewarding to become friends with my new colleagues at work and to have their respect.

Then there were times when I had a good day at work, but driving home I suddenly burst into tears, and cried all the way home. I wondered, *Why am I working?* and the answer was: so I can go home, pay the grocery bills, the utilities, the mortgage; and I'm doing that so I can go to work . . . it was an endless round sometimes.

Then I decided my social life was dull; my personal life was dull. I had nobody that I could relate to personally. *But if I have a dull life, it's got to be my fault,* I thought. *Nobody can change it but me. So I'm going to make it interesting.*

Rose: There was one particularly hard year in my life—1982. For some reason, several people felt it was their mission in life to inform me that I was too difficult to be with or too hard to understand, so they just couldn't be with me any more. It was horrible.

At that time, it was very helpful to take the Myers-Briggs course—to identify personality *preferences* was life-changing for me. I was able to identify what my inclinations and skills were. (It doesn't mean that I can't do anything besides what comes naturally, but it means that it'll be a little bit harder for me.) And I came to understand that God has created us in different ways, and that just because another person doesn't approach life as I do, that doesn't mean that they're wrong—they're just different, and that's okay. God made me the way I am on purpose, and he made you the way you are on purpose. So I don't have to make any more excuses for myself. I don't have to change you.

I did ask the woman who was leading the course, "What if I can accept myself, but the people around me continue to say, 'You're a jerk—I don't want to be with you'?"

She said something that has changed my life: "Then tell them, 'Well, then you don't get to be with me!'"

I love that! I told my sister she doesn't get to be with me any more. It's been the rule of our relationship for the past couple of years, and everything has been much, much better. No more trying to live up to an impossible ideal—an ideal that *she* has constructed for *my* life. Well, now things seem to have changed. My sister wants to be with me. But I've taken a lot of knocks from her, and I am still fragile. I haven't decided if she gets to be with me yet. I don't know.

LEARNING TO BE CONNECTED

Phyllis, Dorcas and Rose found themselves alone, abandoned, rejected for various reasons; in their isolation they found strength within to cope and, ultimately, to grow.

And while growth can be accomplished under these circumstances, the presence of other women who will serve as guides, friends, and mentors makes the process much easier, and the rewards are greater.

Suzanne was greatly influenced by the women's movement, where she learned to think of all women as her sisters:

My mother always talked to her sisters. They were her support, her comfort, her strength. Who in our generation is around her sisters—who even has a sister to talk to? We women are in this thing together. And when we share information, when we console each other, encourage each other, talk to each other, we get stronger. We get powerful. Women are sisters to one another.

Several women experienced personal break-throughs when they caught onto their connectedness with one another:

Barbara: For most of my life, I felt that everyone else knew what they were doing; that they were confident and competent. It has taken me a long time to figure out that there's a lot of child in all of us. We're scared, and we don't have a perfect handle on everything. And the more I've been able to say that, to talk about how I feel, the more I am able to ring a responsive chord in other people. They are able to share their fears and doubts. We're all in this together. I'm not the only one who's struggling.

This realization makes me so much more comfortable with other people. I don't feel so intimidated. The fears that are within me are part of the human condition. This has given me the freedom in relationships to see beyond exteriors.

Sue Ellen: One day when I was really down about my foster children, a friend of mine called and said, "I'm coming over, and I'm bringing lunch."

And I said, "No, no, I'm fine; that's all right, don't bother," but she didn't listen to me. She came anyway, with chicken soup. We talked for a couple of hours. I'm usually the one baking cookies and making meals for other people. I don't like to be emotionally dependent on my friends—I'd rather be able to handle everything myself. But when women do these sorts of things for each other, there's a bonding. Once I've done something helpful for another person, we are immediately connected to each other. I love that.

Robin: When Richard and I were going through a bad time, I sought out someone that I could talk to. I searched and searched because I wanted it to be someone who loved Richard as much as she loved me. And I found a really wonderful woman who reassured me. She told me that she and her husband had gone through a bad time, too, but now they had a really strong relationship. And it helped me understand that these bad times in a marriage are not failure; they're difficulties, but they're not the end of the world.

Linda: I was helped to be real as a woman, a wife, a mother, by a friendship I had with a woman. She gave me permission to relax, to explore who I was, because she was doing that. She would just listen and encourage me to really feel what I was saying, to get in touch with the anger and dissatisfaction I had—the disparity between the image I was trying to live up to and who I really was. So, her loving me for who I really was made me feel better so that I could forget about all that other garbage.

Hazel: Women of my generation think that the younger generation is too powerful for them. They're afraid of the younger people. But everywhere I go, young women ask me, "Why don't older women teach us? Why don't they give us their wisdom?"

The older women believe that they don't have anything to share, maybe because they don't know anything about computer chips! But that's not true. The older women *do* have something to teach, and the younger women have this tremendous need to learn from them. They don't know

about computers, they don't have advanced degrees, but that's not what's important anyway.

It's the *wisdom* they have! And we can't afford to let that wisdom that they have gained
through their lifetimes and that was passed down
to them by other women die with them!

Hazel's observations didn't end there; during my
interview with her she gave me a personal challenge: to
be a strong Christian woman, a role model that
younger women can look up to.

What? I'm not old enough to be another woman's
guide! I'm the one who needs to learn from older,
mature, confident women like Hazel.

Fine, said Hazel. Keep on learning from older
women. But also realize that you are already an "older
woman" to many of the younger women in your
church. They are looking at your marriage, your home,
your parenting, your work and your faith. What do
they see? Do they see commitment and perseverance?
Constancy and concern? What wisdom are you willing
to impart to others?

LEARNING WHAT GOD EXPECTS

As she wrestles with what the church expects, what
the neighbors expect, what society expects, what her
husband and children expect, and what she herself
expects—the Christian woman must grapple with the
most important expectation of all. She must ask herself, "What does God expect of me?"

Many of the women I talked to asked this question
only in the most general terms; identifying themselves
as Christian women, they pointed to Scripture as providing God's expectation for human beings. Others
were more in touch with particulars—with what God

wanted to see happening in their lives specifically. But specific or general, they all spoke of discerning God's expectations as a learning process, a journey of discovery. And although some spoke of God himself as inscrutable, they all believed that his will (call it his plan) could be found and understood.

Eva: I am restless and bored with navel examination. It doesn't honor God's plan and his grace. It's people he's put in my path that are determining where I go, not an understanding of my past. Every experience has tenderized me, given me compassion and insight. And they're valuable experiences to that extent. But the past can't be allowed to rule my life.

It's no gift to go through life without bumps. The hard experiences in my life have been school for me. I've been doing classes on death and dying, working in a hospice for AIDS patients. My past experiences with suffering have made me a useful individual in these situations. My sister's child is dying and because of my training and the tenderness I've developed throughout my life, I'm able to be very helpful in that situation.

God is sovereign, and everything that comes our way is preparation for . . . who knows what? Something. It's preparation for something.

Irene: When I had my heart attacks, I realized that I was expendable, yet not expendable. The world went on without me, yet God still needed me. I hadn't thought in those terms before. I know that I could have another heart attack today, and I could die. And I can accept that. But until I do die, I know that my work isn't done yet; God wants me alive for some purpose.

Virginia: I picture myself as a watering can, lying on its side next to a garden. God has picked me up, filled me with water, and then poured the water onto the plants in the garden. I'm used in that way. It's nothing that I have on my own, only that I can hold what he puts in me, and then be used to pour it onto others. It has been a big surprise to me that I've been able to help other women the way I have. I never thought I could be used this way. I'm uneducated and untrained. Yet I have a ministry. The Lord still uses ordinary people, and that's exciting.

Tricia: My spiritual life is uneven. I draw close to God, and then I pull away. I take a step forward, then maybe I take two steps backward.

In this, though, I have a sense of anticipation because I think that the Lord has something for me. I don't know what it is, and I don't know if it's something that will happen sooner or later, but I do have this feeling that I'm being prepared for something different. He's going to require something of me, and I'm getting ready for that.

In the past, I've had dreams that had to do with future events. When my dad got sick and died, I could see that a number of experiences and feelings had been working in me to prepare me for that. I believe that there's meaning in what I'm doing now—meaning for the future. Something's going on, even though I don't know where it's going to take me.

I'm to the place now where I can live with it if other people are disappointed in me. But if I fail to live up to my own standards, or fail to accomplish what I think is important, or don't meet my personal expectations . . . that's a whole lot harder. I'm learning to deal with this. I'm growing up.

This self-acceptance goes up and down, and almost always in proportion to my relationship with God. To be so concerned with *my* expectations for *my* life is a form of self-centeredness.

When I get frustrated with myself, or disappointed in myself, it's because I'm focusing on me. I should be focusing on God. If I focus on him, I can accept my own shortcomings a whole lot better.

Other people have needs and in comparison to mine, their needs are usually greater. *That's* something worthwhile to focus on. *That's* a better placement of priorities. After all, whose glory is my life for? I need to constantly remind myself that I'm here to live for God, not for me.

Nedra: It's been very healthy for me to let go of some of the expectations I've had for my Christian life—that I will attend a certain church, do certain things, feel a certain way. My walk now is much less conditional on these sorts of observances and much more centered around my love for God and his love for me.

In the past, I fulfilled these outward obligations so well that I actually thought I didn't have any sin. When I was a child, I'd sit in church, and when there was some call to repentance, I'd sit there and think, *Well, I've obeyed all the commandments, I've done all the dos and none of the don'ts—let's see, there must be something I could confess . . . well, whatever it is, Lord, forgive me.*

I'd fulfilled all the expectations, done them all. I couldn't think of where I might be falling short.

And that's still an easy attitude for me to fall into. This prideful attitude of having done all the right things and stayed clear of all the wrong ones. But I'm changing. I'm realizing that being a Christian is more than living up to the expectations of the church, my parents, even the Bible. It's a love relationship.

Karen: I can look at Proverbs 31 as an impossible dream or a recipe for a nervous breakdown. Or I can see it as a composite of all Christian women. I can't be everything in Proverbs 31, but I can be some of those things, and other women can be other things. And together there is a picture of what Christian womanhood can be and should be.

So it's okay for me to be at home with my children now and to look after the children of friends so that they can have jobs. It's okay for them to work. People should be allowed to be who they are, because God made them who they are.

Rose: God has given me talents, and I've buried them because that was what my husband told me to do; the church told me to bury my talent because they needed help with Vacation Bible School. I've tried to be a cooperative wife and reliable church member.

But then I realized that I'm going to be held accountable for how I have used my talents—not Paul and not my church. If I say to God, "I couldn't do my life's mission because my husband said I couldn't," then will God say, "Oh, yes, that's the one excuse that I'll accept"? I doubt it! When I realized that I was in a position of disobedience, I realized that I had to change.

This realization helped me decide that I would do everything in my power to do what God wants me to do.

LEARNING TO HEAL

My favorite light bulb joke: How many psychologists does it take to change a light bulb? Only one . . . but the light bulb has to really *want* to change.

It's the act of will that brings about change for most of us—if not for light bulbs. Jesus asked the blind beggar on the road to Jericho, "What do you want me to do for you?"

"Lord, I want to see," replied the beggar.

"Receive your sight," said Jesus. "Your faith has healed you."

This story is found in Luke; it was Luke, the physician, who recorded it and captured an important truth in the telling. Jesus didn't go around healing people without their consent; rather, he acted upon their expression of need and their willingness to accept healing.

Two women spoke to me at some length about their experience of seeking and receiving healing. Neither feels that she has come out on the other side of her difficulty or that she can speak as a conqueror. Both are still very much in the midst of healing.

> **Angela:** My depression about my inability to be the perfect mother cycled around PMS (premenstrual syndrome). I could cope most of the time because I really did love my kids. But when I was in the throes of PMS, I would get very melancholy, be critical of my kids, critical of my marriage, and I had a loss of faith.
>
> I would fantasize that I'd leave my family and go to New York City and live *there* in despair.

Sometimes it seemed a very sensible thing to do—to be anonymously ruined in that city. There seemed no other way out.

I remember being upstairs, in a corner, in the fetal position, crying and crying and crying. I wished someone would see how miserable I was and put me in a hospital. I never did entertain the idea of suicide, so I never worried that I would hurt myself. But I did *try* to cross the line into psychosis, but I just couldn't make it.

I spent quite a bit of time on the phone to friends who lived in other parts of the country, crying to them. One friend recommended that I go to a Spiritual Directions workshop, and I quickly gave all the reasons why I couldn't go: no one to watch the children, no money, no time, and so on. And she answered, "When are you going to be worth it?"

That blew my mind. When would I start taking care of myself, and working through some of my old issues, and trying to find a way out of the mess I was in?

So I went; it was the beginning of healing. I began to image wholeness. I resolved a lot of issues with my mother.

I was creating some bad stuff at home with my own children, and much of it had to do with my own parental issues. I didn't want my kids to show their feelings because I had so many unexpressed emotions myself. I felt a lot of guilt about my parenting failures.

But I was told at this workshop to relax about that because the unresolved issues that my kids had with me would be their way of growing. For example, a couple of years ago my daughter, Jenny, and I were driving in the car, and she was reading a book about wildflowers. All of a sudden, she started to cry. I didn't know what was happening. I asked her what was wrong, and she told me that several summers ago when we were real busy building our house, she had brought me a handful of wildflowers as a gift, and I had told her, "Oh, those are just weeds."

I felt guilty, of course. But the good part was that she told me about it, and we talked and I asked for her forgiveness and assured her that she didn't deserve that kind of comment. I told her that I really did love her. That interaction was better for our relationship than if nothing at all had happened—or than if I had thanked her and hugged her when she brought me the flowers all those years ago. There was a purpose to it, not an intentional one, but a purpose anyway, and it brought about healing from my weakness.

Cheryl: I kept the rules for a lot of years, and you're catching me at the time when I'm questioning some of them. Like tithing. I've tithed all my Christian life; I've always been told that if you tithe, the Lord will bless you financially.

Well, I'm not tithing any more, and you know what? I'm better off than I ever was. Now, I'm a single mother with five kids. When we came to this city, we didn't have one stick of furniture except my desk. We all slept on the floor, we ate on the floor, we had nothing. I've furnished our house from top to bottom, bought new beds for everybody, done it all.

I've broken every rule. I'm not into keeping the law anymore. I'm not saying that the disciplines are bad; they're not bad. But they're not something we have to do so that God will love us.

This is about a lot of things, not just money. In our churches we hear, "This happened, then that happened." And over time you come to understand it means, "Do this, and then God will do that." Give a tithe, he'll make you rich; read your Bible, you'll get wisdom; pray and you'll be happy; keep this law and God will like you. Everything will work out okay for you if you do these things the right way.

The worse I acted after I got my divorce, the neater God was—the more loving he was, the more caring he was. I've met the most caring, loving, committed, genuine people. Real people who love God and love me—people who are not clinging to a legalistic understanding of God in hopes that they can persuade him to give them something they want, but people who are completely trustful and trusting.

Did you need to test God?

Oh, yes, I can remember doing some things and thinking, "Okay, God, love me now. Look at what I'm doing and love me." And he did. I'm not saying that we should go out and sin so that God will love us. I'm not saying that. But I had kept the law so perfectly all those years I was married, and God only became real to me when I let go of all that stuff and let him take me right where I was. Now, I'm forming a real friendship with him, and it's an honest relationship.

When you move away from the law, there's always the danger of going too far the other way—which I have done. And I'm working on some of my compulsive, excessive behaviors. But I'm doing this because I choose to, not because anyone is telling me to, and not because I had to do it in order for God to like me. It's a heart attitude.

Like . . .

I'm drinking, and I'm drinking for all the wrong reasons. I started because it helped me lighten up, it made it a little easier to be around my kids. And I've come to depend on it, and I need to stop. It's not like I'm chugging hard liquor or something—I'm drinking wine—but it has come to be something that I really look forward to and something I rely on.

After so many years of not having my wants and needs met, I have to learn how to meet them in appropriate ways and not to go overboard indulging my whims. It's hard for me to say no to myself these days because I've done that for so long. I need to separate the legitimate needs from the bogus needs. In a way, it was easier when I had all the rules to follow; I didn't have to work so hard at knowing what was right and wrong.

I'm looking at life the way it really is. But I wake up each morning not expecting life to be perfect. I don't expect it to be easy. So the little things become very precious. I can enjoy a walk with a friend, watching my kids' eyes light up if they get a new pair of shoes.

It doesn't take much to make me happy. I love toys, I love balloons. I'm very thankful: for my job, for my friends, for my kids, for every little thing I get. I don't ever want to take for granted—not ever—the little things God does for me.

I can't say that for my friends who have had pretty easy lives. They expect a lot of God, and they get so mad at him when he doesn't come through! I don't expect anything from God; I don't pray much about my needs, because I don't feel he's obligated to do anything. I'm willing to put my life under his control, but he's the one who decides if he'll give me what I think I need.

That's a good place for me because I don't get disappointed like I used to. I still have expectations, but they're not in control. They're getting less and less. I expect my kids and my friends to disappoint me because they're human after all. My disappointments are *my* disappointments, not someone else's fault or failure.

LEARNING TO CONFRONT THE FUTURE

Karen: When I turned thirty, I said, "All right, when I'm forty all my kids are going to be in school full-time, I'm going to be in great physical shape, and I'm going to be working part-time." I turned thirty-nine last week, and I think now, *That's ridiculous, I've got a preschooler, and if I'm going to be in perfect physical shape I'd better get busy.* Really, I'm not good at this long-range goal setting. . . .

When I asked women how far ahead they looked into the future, and what they saw, many were unable to answer the question. When we've had the experience of seeing past goals go unreached, past expectations remain unmet, we're apt to be shy about making further goals and identifying further expectations. Some were consciously taking life one day at a time, nothing more, realizing from past experience that they couldn't hope to function any other way. Many had plans for the future, specific milestones that they were expecting or working toward: becoming a partner in a business, having more children, buying a house, going back to work once the kids are in school, returning to school themselves for further education, having grandchildren. When the future visualized was a pleasant one, they tended to focus on it and work toward it.

When they saw an unpleasant future, they didn't dwell on it.

June: The classic definition of mid-life transition is this: You start looking at how many years you've got left to live as opposed to how many you've lived so far. I've made this transition in the last year.

I realize that my body is changing; it gets tired more easily. How many years of good health are ahead of me? I think about my children's education and how that will be financed. Retirement funds and nest eggs have become important to me.

Marilyn: My middle-age depression doesn't have to do with plans I made that haven't happened, expectations that didn't turn into reality. My depression centers around the fact that now that I'm in middle age, I need to *start* making plans. My future isn't unlimited any more. And I'm going to have to plan out more carefully to accommodate that. Life is no longer limitless possibilities for me.

Irene: When I turned fifty a lot of really neat things started happening for me. It was very unexpected. And who knows what will happen in my sixties? Most of my life, I've expected my life to "wind down" but that hasn't happened. It's still going on, still progressing.

Sandra: There will always be a gap between my expectations and my reality. But I'm feeling better equipped to deal with the gap because I realize that none of us knows what's around the corner. No matter how much we plan, on any level—emotionally, financially, spiritually—there's no guarantee. I've seen too many people whose lives were going one direction and, due to circumstances beyond their control, they were turned around completely.

Maybe this won't help me a lot when the crisis comes. But I think it will, because I've lowered my expectations for the future in my planning. I realize there's only so much I can do to influence my future . . . it's beyond my control.

Barbara: My early orientation, which was not to expect that things will get ever grander and more glorious in my life, is still with me. I don't look ahead to terrific success. I won't be surprised if this business doesn't make it or if my health fails. I know I'll survive any of that. I do have a sense of joy and trust in who God is, but not in what will happen in my personal future.

AND NOW, THE BENEDICTION

Cora: When we say, "What if . . ." that's an expression of our fear. What if my husband leaves me? What if my daughter is on drugs? What if I lose my job?

But it's an act of faith to turn those "what ifs" into "even if." Even if my husband leaves me, even if my daughter is on drugs, even if I lose my job . . . God will love me and I will survive.

CORA'S STORY

Looking back over twenty-five years of marriage, Cora can pinpoint disappointments that have created "a wall of resentment" toward her husband. As she deals with her grief, within the context of her faith and commitment to the marriage, she is finding her security lies with God.

When my mother died, my father remarried. He was very anxious that we bond as a family, so he did things like asking me to call my stepmother "Mom." I can see, looking back, that the remarriage was a very difficult thing for me, and in a way I closed my heart to him when he remarried. I felt rejected; I thought that his love for me had been replaced by his love for her. I felt her need to be called "Mom" was more important to him than my need to save that word for my real mother.

No one in my family openly expressed love and affection. I didn't think that anyone loved me or cared about me. I cried every day.

EVEN IF

I didn't put a lot of thought into getting married. When I met Alan, it seemed right. I knew I loved him, and he was responsible, so when he asked me to marry him I thought, *That's what you do when you grow up,* and I accepted. I know I'm Pollyannish in nature. I probably just thought it would be wonderful. I thought, *Now I'll have love.*

Was it what you had hoped?

At first. But then some hurtful things happened.

When I got pregnant for the first time, I was excited and nervous. But when I passed the due date for delivery, Alan decided to go ahead to a meeting in another city. I was so hurt. What it said to me was that he cared more for his work than he did for me. My condition, our new baby . . . they weren't as important.

Our son was born without him. Alan chose to be gone. I've cried buckets over that experience. God's been healing me in the past year, but it's been so difficult. Our first child, something special, something to experience together—and Alan wasn't there.

He's loved by his employees and his co-workers and business associates—yet he hasn't been there for me and for our kids.

I wanted to go to a marriage seminar. I thought we really needed it for our marriage. I told Alan what it was, and why I wanted to go, and why I thought it was important for us. And he said no. He had to work that weekend. Well, I didn't just let it go at that, as I've done for twenty-five years. I persisted and told him that he could get someone else to work for him over the weekend. I wanted him to reconsider. But he said no.

I really grieved that answer. And I let him see me grieve. It's not that I wanted to manipulate him with my tears, but I wanted to be honest with him; I didn't want to stuff my grief in a drawer so he didn't have to see it. But still he said that he had a commitment to his job, that he expected his employees to give 100 percent and he should do the same.

I was so disappointed. His refusal to go to the marriage conference reopened the old wound. Something died in me, emotionally. I've been unable to have any kind of emotional response to Alan since then.

When I died to Alan emotionally, I came to the place where I said, "I simply cannot pretend any longer. I cannot pretend that I love him, that I feel something there, because there isn't." I pulled away. I didn't try to be nice, loving, communicative. I quit making love. I didn't think he loved me or cared for me, so I didn't think there was any reason to have sex.

I knew that this was no way for a good, godly wife to act, but I couldn't do it any other way. I had to feel my pain, and I had to let Alan get mad—which he did. He got very mad. But I didn't want to manipulate and control him by being nice, by complying, by submitting. All those things looked good on the surface, but underneath I knew that doing those things was just a way of getting that man to stay with me.

I went to a counselor, and I asked him what I was going to do with this huge wall of resentment I had against my husband. He said that I needed to figure out what it was that I believed but that wasn't actually true. If I could identify my wrong beliefs, the wall of resentment would come tumbling down. I wouldn't have to do anything further about it.

One of my erroneous beliefs was that I could look to Alan for my personal security, that he could give me the life I need. So I was looking to Alan, demanding and expecting that he would give me that deep-down fulfillment and security I needed. I was trying to buy my security from Alan, doing everything I could to make him stay in the marriage, making me feel secure.

Once I saw what I was doing and identified this wrong belief—that any person could do that for me—it really did help with that wall of resentment.

Previously, if I didn't want to make love, I did it anyway because I thought, *If I don't, he'll leave me.* I was trying to buy security and acceptance by having sex with him whenever he wanted, regardless of my own feelings.

Alan has needed sex often—at least it seems often to me—a few times a week. And our physical relationship has been good, it's been satisfying. But I was selling myself. I've quit doing that. He pouted and got angry at first, but that's okay. I need to feel that when we're having sex, it's an expression of our love, not something I do to ward off rejection.

I never would divorce Alan. I never would, never. I intend to remain faithful to my vows and faithful to God in this relationship. But I don't think that Alan believes this about me. I think he can see me leaving. And it's this thought of what his life would be like without his wife, without his children, that has really shaken him up. He's taken stock. And he's become much more aware of himself, much more in touch with his own loneliness. He's confronting his fear—his fear of losing me, losing his family.

I gave up control of trying to keep our marriage together. I decided to let God control it, decided to let him keep it together if that's what he wanted.

I said, "Even if." Even if it's not a happy marriage. Even if Alan leaves me, even if it all falls apart . . . I'm not going to manipulate any more.

Every time I've felt the pain, experienced the reality, looked at what's going on inside of me, and asked God to be present in that, I've become more healthy, more whole.

Alan and I are in process now. I can see something I couldn't see before: he really does care. Otherwise, he wouldn't respond at all.

We have a long way to go in working on our marriage. But that's okay. We've been married for twenty-five years and it's possible that we'll be married for another twenty-five years. Things aren't great, but I'm not going to panic because we don't get everything worked out this week. I can allow it to happen in God's time. Probably our relationship is the best it has ever been; it's more honest. But we're not out of the woods, by a long shot. And it's certainly not what it should be, or what it can be.

DESTROYING WRONG BELIEFS

Another problem I've had is my performance orientation. I used to strive for perfect grades. I kept my house absolutely immaculate, I was a perfect wife to Alan. I thought that doing all this would give me life. That being needed gave me life. This came from my underlying belief that I was not loved, and that I was not worth loving. So I did all things in order to manipulate people into loving me.

The more I grow in the security of God's Word, the more I understand what he's written in his Word—I am loved, I am loved with an everlasting love, I am loved so much that his son died for me, I am worthy—the more I'm able to rest in his love.

One time I heard God say to me, "I love you. I love you if you do nothing more than sit in that chair. I love you if you never do another thing in your life. I love you, regardless of what you do or don't do. I love you."

But I'm still confronting wrong beliefs. Deep down inside, I believe that imperfection equals rejection. I need to keep aware of the lies that I believe in my heart; I need to let go of them at a deep level and let go of the pain connected with some of those wrong beliefs. I need to reject the falsehoods and embrace the truth, so that I don't have so many demands or expectations that I'm placing on myself. I can relax and rest in God's love.

One of the major things God is doing in my life is destroying my image of what a Christian woman is: my good girl image, my good Christian image, my godly woman image. Of course he wants righteousness and goodness, but he's also having me face up to the fact that I'm human, and that human is okay—even with the imperfections. Even when we were sinners he died for us—that's how he feels about us, sin and all. He values us as human beings. There's an intrinsic value he sees, a value I don't always see.

I've been a people-pleaser all my life. I've been a good girl, a perfect wife, a good Christian.

One of the things God has let me do in the past couple years is just be more honest about my humanness, more real as a person. I've let God see my anger in prayer or as I write to him. And when I share with other women or when I'm speaking, I'm totally honest about my humanity and imperfections. And this is being very helpful to people. They have the misconception that my life is perfect, that I don't have their struggles. But as I share my struggles and imperfections, they open up to me and they become receptive to God's work and his healing in a way that they wouldn't have been otherwise.

CHAPTER SEVEN

Body, Mind, and Spirit

To the person with a toothache, even if the world is tottering, there is nothing more important than a visit to a dentist.
—George Bernard Shaw

*M*y own toothaches have never seemed less painful comparing them to others' agonies. The labor of childbirth wasn't any easier knowing that some women have it much worse. A sleepless night with a crying baby isn't more restful if I reflect that at least it's not the *true* colic of my friend's three-month-old. My painful incision feels no better if I reflect that twenty-five years ago I would have died without it, as many did.

No, if you've got a toothache, the world's problems seem to fade into the throbbing discomfort. Pain is personal and insistent—it must be dealt with, it must be relieved.

I talked to women who are coping with serious physical, mental, and emotional illnesses and disabilities. Some are forced to spend nearly all their energy dealing with their disease; others have found ways to go on with a normal life in spite of poor health. A few have been blessed with healing, and it's changed their entire lives.

PREGNANCY, CHILDBIRTH, PMS, AND ALL THAT

> **Sue Ellen:** I loved being pregnant. I felt so feminine. It felt like an adventure, something special.

Some of the women I talked to reported normal, uneventful pregnancies and deliveries. One said she felt like the Virgin Mary when she was pregnant; many had wonderful birth experiences: reasonable labor, healthy babies, healthy moms.

Others—significantly, these were most often the ones who are only a few years away from the experience—reported disappointments.

> **Anita:** I've had difficulties with bleeding during a couple of my pregnancies. One time was particularly scary: after lovemaking, I started to bleed heavily. And there was a part of me that saw my husband as this penetrator who caused pain and danger. It was traumatic for me and for Chuck. Lovemaking has never been carefree during pregnancy.
>
> When I came home with the news that I was a few weeks pregnant with our fourth child, Chuck said, "Oh-oh, it's not a vagina anymore; it's The Birth Canal!" It was hard for him to relate to me in an erotic way when I was pregnant.
>
> I went for months without having intercourse. During this time, I didn't have much perspective on the issue. I didn't know it was a temporary state, and that now, years later, sex would be great. If I had been able to believe

things would get better, that pregnancy, child-birth, nursing and the chronic fatigue that goes with those things would pass someday, I would have been more at peace about having infrequent sex.

Sharon: The hardest time in my life was when Garrett was born. Michelle was two (there were three older children as well). During the final stages of my pregnancy I was diagnosed as having a rare form of breast cancer.

I had Garrett, an induced delivery. Then ten days later I had a mastectomy. I came home from the hospital, and my mother was there for a couple of weeks, holding things together. But then she left, and things got really difficult.

I had a newborn and was recovering from major surgery. We found out that our two-year-old might be autistic. Ken was out of the house all that time. Michelle kept trying to escape from the house; she'd slip out of the door without any clothes on.

This sounds terrible.

I remember seeing friends at parties or church, and they'd ask how I was doing, and I would say, "I really think that I might have died and gone to hell."

What happened?

It just got better. It got better with time. I became stronger, physically, and the children grew out of their stages.

What about now?

I learned that I won't always be here for my kids. Children take their mother for granted. They assume that she'll be there to look after them and pick up the pieces. But I realized that they all need to learn how to be sensitive to me and also how to take care of themselves more. What if something should happen to me?

Has that been a lasting change?

I'm afraid not. It was more like them rising to the occasion because of a crisis. They definitely tend to relapse. But *I* do look after myself more than I used to.

I have a friend who, whenever she sees me, asks, "Sharon, what are you doing to take care of yourself?" She doesn't ask about the children, or the house, or what Ken's doing. I report to her. She knows that no one is going to all of a sudden start looking after me; I have to do that for myself.

What do you do for yourself?

I force myself to get with other women as much as I can. I've been going out a lot at night instead of hanging around the house. We put the kids to bed real early, so I do have free time in the evenings.

What about physical things?

That's really important. I have to walk at least a mile a day. If I don't get at least that much exercise I crash around 6:30, and get really impatient with everybody. If I can have a walk, my energy lasts a lot longer.

Marsha: I suffer from PMS—premenstrual syndrome. I hate this feeling of being torn apart. There is a part of me that is at the mercy of my hormones; I become depressed and have horrible feelings of utter despair. But that can't really be me! I never felt that way before Stephanie was born, and now I feel that way before my periods start. So I visualize it as this inside/outside force that is messing me up. I do understand that it's not going to be permanent, but on the other hand, it is my body and it is part of who I am. I feel torn.

My own two pregnancies were exciting—and dangerous. Whenever I heard someone reflect on the trauma of childbirth, I bonded to them immediately; we became sisters-in-arms, soldiers in the battle to bear children and live to tell the story.

There are ties that bind, too, for women who fight to conceive.

"If I Could Just Bear a Child"

Bette: We'd been married five years, still no children. We went through all kinds of tests, and the doctor said he didn't see any reason why we couldn't have children. We decided to adopt our first child and have our own later.

We adopted our first child, but I didn't feel complete. I told myself that if I could just bear a child, I'd be a whole woman. So I went through more tests—I really went big-time with the tests. Nothing happened, never any pregnancies.

For years I fostered that lie: that if I could just have a child, I'd be a complete woman. Apparently, I wasn't alone in thinking this.

We had moved to a new city, and a woman from church was over at our house. By then, we had three adopted children. She sat me down and said, "I need, as your friend, to talk to you about something. I think you should realize that every man needs to have his own child."

I was overwhelmed; I think it was the most horrible experience of my whole life. The fact that she called herself my friend, yet didn't understand how much I wanted my own child, how I'd gone through all those tests, how alone I felt during the tests: to go into the doctor's office for tests, when everyone else in the waiting room is pregnant. It's so humiliating. It's degrading in a sense.

I got sick to my stomach. The baby was in his bedroom, and I said, "I think I hear the baby." He was asleep in his bed, but I pinched him until he woke up and cried so that woman would leave.

That was one of the biggest disappointments of my life. To have this person I thought was a friend, and then hear her say to me, "You're not good enough. You're not a real woman. You're a reject."

James said, "You can't afford to have a friend like that." And I said, "Yes, but she's in all my groups at church," and he said, "No, I'm serious. You cannot afford to have a friend like that. Disassociate yourself from that relationship." And that, basically, is what I did. But it was so sad for me, that she didn't care to understand what I was going through. I don't know how much she could have known; maybe you have to go through that kind of hell to sympathize with someone who is there.

I think friends can do the most by walking with people when they're going through difficulties. I would have given anything for a friend who would have gone to my doctor's appointments with me. Some did offer but I'm a strong person and my first reaction was to say, "No, I'm okay." But I did need someone to watch the other kids while I was having the tests, and I used my friends more as babysitters than as escorts.

I don't know when I came to terms with infertility. I suppose it happened over a period of years. When I went in for my forty-year checkup, my doctor asked me what I was going to do about preventing pregnancy. I told him it had never been a problem, that I'd been trying for years to get pregnant. But he told me I was at the perfect age to get pregnant; the change-of-life pregnancy often happens to couples who have never had a pregnancy.

I went home and said, "James, get fixed." I didn't want a pregnancy at that stage of my life.

So you really had come a long way.

That's right. I had enjoyed every one of my five kids, but I was also enjoying the new freedom of *not* having young children. I didn't need to have a pregnancy to feel like a real woman.

Different ones who can't have children have asked me, "How did you get over it?" We had been living overseas, and I got really sick. During a year-and-a-half illness, I developed this realization that I wasn't alone. I could see where the Lord was in all of that. He was beside me all the time I was sick. In that, I began to be able to say, "God, whatever *you* want is okay."

I've been told, all my life, that I should turn myself over to God. But I'd never really grappled with that issue before my illness. It was then that I could say, honestly, if I get pregnant it's fine. If I don't get pregnant it's fine. I didn't have to prove who I was by a pregnancy.

EXPECTATIONS OF HEALTH, REALITIES OF ILLNESS

Irene: One of my expectations was that I would always be healthy and strong because I grew up that way. My mother died when she was thirty-four, and from the time that I was twenty-five to about thirty-five, it was always amazing to me that she had died and I was alive.

Then, about seven years ago, I had three mini-strokes. I couldn't read numbers straight, I couldn't write a sentence without misspelling five words, I couldn't do anything right. Then, a couple years after that, I went into a clinical depression that lasted for two years. I'm a pretty "up" person most of the time, but that depression was a real blow. I could not get out of it. I prayed, I confessed, I went through therapy, all kinds of medical checks. But I could not get out of it. Eventually, it was found that my body wasn't producing the appropriate chemicals, and now I'm on medication that takes care of it.

It was good, though, for me to understand what happens to other people who get depressed. When you're an "up" person, as I am, it's sometimes hard to understand others who aren't that way.

Two years ago, I had a heart attack, here at work. Then I had another heart attack in the same week, and by-pass surgery right after that. It was another major blow.

Still, I expect to be very healthy for the rest of my life!

If you expect health, it takes a while to get used to the idea that health may never be yours—Irene, in spite of it all, hopes for health.

Vicki and Caroline are both young women in their thirties who have had to deal with severe health problems: Vicki is struggling with chronic illness, and Caroline has had a string of surgeries and infections in the past four years.

Vicki: Statistically, families fall apart when the wife gets seriously ill. Most men can't deal with it. I belong to a support group of women with my disease, and I've seen that their husbands have taken off. I'm grateful that in our marriage illness has made us think more critically about how we treat each other. It's been a reminder that we're mortal, and that if we aren't careful we'll take each other for granted—and our children, too. We've been jolted into realizing that nothing lasts forever, and my own life may be shorter than I had once thought. We've begun to think about each other daily.

Because Tony and I had made serious efforts to communicate when I was well, we were able to keep it up when I got sick. I never felt I had to hide it from him if I was angry or upset or depressed. It's okay to express those things with him.

So often it's the dumb things that irk me, not the big, life-threatening things. For example, I have to stay out of the sun. Going to the beach means number thirty-five sunscreen and a wide-brimmed hat and long sleeves and trying to find a tree to sit under. My hair is patchy underneath, I have bald spots. I gain weight on my medication, and it's really hard to lose it. I feel guilty. I'm not the person that Tony married; I'm sick.

He tells me that the way I looked was what attracted him to me in the first place. But now, that's not the only thing that he likes about me. There's more there. Even though things aren't exactly the same, that's okay. In the past, he has encouraged me and told me about all the things that he loved about me—and my looks were only one of those things. So I know, now, that when I look bad because of my disease, I haven't lost the only thing he cares about. I can remember back to when I was healthy and know that even then there was more.

When I got sick, I received a barrage of information from friends and family about how I could be well—by taking vitamins or reading a certain book or going on a special diet or thinking positively or whatever.

I had a chance to talk to Joni Eareckson Tada, and she told me about how it feels to be in some sort of religious gathering where people take the stage and preach that if you have faith you can be healed, you can have anything you want. Or that if you were right with the Lord only good things would happen to you. Disease is caused by unconfessed sin. That sort of thing. And there she sits, and it hasn't been in God's plan to heal her, at least not now.

One woman sent me a tape series that basically said I was sick because I had unconfessed sin in my life—it was horrible. Because of Joni's experience, I could tell myself, "Don't worry about that—it just isn't true." I know that God intends for me to be healthy, and I know that I will be someday, but what I don't know is if I will get health in this life, or in the life to come. That's up to God.

Our children, even though they are small, have come to have a more real faith in God because of my illness. They know God isn't the bubble-gum machine in the sky. They know what illness and pain are, and they know about prayer, and they know that you don't always get what you ask for. God is there, he loves us, he's sent his son to die for us . . . but that doesn't make life easy.

Caroline: I've wakened up to the fact that things can't be perfect. I was in top physical condition before and during my first pregnancy. And then came the delivery; hour after hour of hard pushing and still I couldn't get the baby out. I had to have a Caesarean.

Then I had abdominal surgery during my second pregnancy—possible uterine cancer—and then more surgery two months after the second baby was born by Caesarean. I was in the hospital for almost two weeks after that surgery with a toxic-shock type thing; I had to give up nursing, and, one year later, I'm still wiped out because of it.

I've been told I had these physical problems because I wasn't taking the right vitamin tonic, because my husband was neglecting me, because I tried to do too much and didn't take care of myself. I've quit looking for reasons. I don't want to think about it any more. And I haven't thought a lot about what God was trying to show me because I'm not sure that he *was* trying to show me anything.

I don't believe it's some spiritual problem showing itself in my body, I don't believe that there's anything I could have done to prevent any of this. It's bad luck and I'm learning to accept that. I can also accept it because those were all things that came out of having children, and I'm so happy to have gotten two healthy babies out of the thing that I can honestly say I'd do it again. I've known what it's like to lie in the hospital and be pretty sure that I won't see my children again; I know what it's like to pass out from pain. So I've learned to accept my present level of health, which isn't great, as something I can live with. Even though it frustrates me, even though I wonder if it will ever end, even though I know that something's still wrong with me, I hold onto the fact that I'm not in pain. I'm not hemorrhaging. I don't have a raging fever, a high white blood count. I won't die today.

Four years ago, I expected to have perfect weight, perfect body tone, a concave stomach, and perfect health. Now, I'm satisfied that I can get on with my life if I can remember that today I'm not going to die.

THE STRUGGLE FOR A LIFE

Carla: I was sexually abused by my grandfather from the time I was three until I was eight or nine. It is the backdrop of everything that has happened to me since that time.

I've had eating disorders since I was fourteen. It started with bulimia and then progressed to anorexia nervosa. By the time I was in college, it had gotten very serious. I attended a conservative Christian college in the South.

Were they supportive of you during this time?

Uh, no. Not very supportive. I will say that they did finally take one important step: They had me hospitalized—but that was when I was losing a pound or two a day; throwing up four, five, or six times a day. I was so depressed I couldn't get out of bed.

There was not a lot of understanding. For example, I was a nursing student, and I remember the last day I was at school before I was hospitalized. I knew I was getting very, very sick, and I told my nursing instructor that I wouldn't be there the next day, and she asked, "Why?" That's when I had lost forty pounds in three months. I weighed just about a hundred pounds and fainted whenever I stood up. And she asked, "Why?" She was medically trained and everything, but she was more interested in me being a good nursing student than in me as a person.

The expectation was that if you were a student, you were a fine Christian with no problems. Everyone was fairly oblivious to problems; they sure weren't looking for hurts in other people. Until I was really dying, and it was staring them in the face, they took no notice.

Now there were some people who kept up with me through my hospital treatment, who would come and visit me and support me. And some friends who came to visit said, "I really didn't know what this was, I didn't know what you were going through." And out of that there was a chance to do some real bonding, to build and rebuild relationships that had suffered during my illness.

After I had completed treatment, I became more open about the problems in my life. I began to tell people about the sexual abuse I'd had as a child, and about my home life, and my bulimia and anorexia, and my depression and suicidal thoughts. They were blown away. This was not what they wanted to hear from a student at a Christian college.

There was one professor who came to visit me in the hospital. She sat there and said, "You don't look happy." Happy? I was almost dead! And then she said, "Let's just pray about this that it will get better." As though she could just fix everything with her prayers.

She asked, "Have you been praying?" No. "Have you been reading the Scripture?" No.

She believed that if I'd been praying and reading my Bible, this never would have happened to me. A lot of people had this opinion. "Carla, spiritually you haven't been right with God, and that's the problem here."

But you see, I hadn't been right with God because I'd been so emotionally ill.

My parents were the same way.

Had you told them about the sexual abuse from your grandfather?

I didn't tell anyone. He had told me that if I told my parents, they wouldn't love me any more. In fact, as the years went on, I pretty much forgot about it. It was there, but I suppressed it. Five weeks into treatment, I started to have terrible nightmares, I thought I was going to go crazy. It all came back, and I had to face it.

How have you faced it? Is he still alive, and does that help you deal with what happened?

I pray he'll die. I remember what happened. I've confronted him, though he denies everything. He says, "How could you think that? I'd never do anything to hurt you." He won't talk about it or look at it with me. Yet still, last Christmas, he grabbed my breasts. I'm twenty-five years old and he's still doing the same stuff. No change. When I tell him that's not appropriate, he looks at me like I'm crazy.

My first two years at college, I was the perfect Christian student. I did my daily devotions, I prayed, I went to chapel, I attended classes. I did it all by the book. But then, when I began to have a lot of problems, I needed counseling. I became manic-depressive, and my eating disorder got very serious. There was simply no understanding.

I'm not saying I understood it all myself. I had these mood swings, I was seeing a psychiatrist, I was taking medications, I was also practicing "cutting"—it's another addiction I have: I can take a razor blade and make a big slash on my skin, and I don't feel any pain emotionally for a week.

I know this is bizarre, but it seems to me that nobody even had a *desire* to understand. I was just weird. I just had these terrible problems.

I remember asking someone, "What can I do to get well?" And they said, "Boy, I don't know. How's your walk with God?" Well, it was horrible. I didn't even know if God loved me.

Finally, in my last year of college, I was taking a seminary-level theology class. I went into my professor's office, sobbing, and said, "I don't know if I'm a Christian. I don't know if God loves me."

He was a wonderful man. He said, "Of all the people in this university, you might be the most honest Christian I've met so far." *That* gave me some hope.

How do you feel about that college experience, as you look back?

Angry. Real angry. Because, of all the places in the world where I should have been accepted, I wasn't. I was a freak. You would think that on the campus of a Christian university, there would be love and compassion and understanding, not ignorance and denial and fear.

How has it left your faith?

My faith was shattered. But that conversation I had with my professor was a point where I could start rebuilding from the base: that God is love and I am loved. But I've had to start from the beginning, from almost nothing. And it's slow. In Sunday school terms, I'm about where I was in second grade—with just the very basics.

So much has been in my head. I've got a degree in Bible yet I'm still struggling with the basic concepts of who God is, and that he can be there for me when I'm in trouble, that he's the answer, but he's not a "fix." My spirituality is real important to me, and I know that's where answers lie, but I feel too tentative because I've been so badly burned. I'm slow to believe what I hear or read because I think that an uncritical attitude toward other people's theologies and theories precipitated my own emotional and physical crisis.

It was important to have that professor tell me that doubts were normal, and that my worth wasn't tied up with my emotional health, that I could have this illness and still be loved by God. I could be a mental patient in a mental hospital and still call myself a Christian. I had always thought that Christians didn't have problems. Well, *I* had problems, so I thought I couldn't be a Christian. To find out that I could be a Christian with problems was a big revelation to me. I used to look at these girls I lived with in the dorm and think, *Boy, they're so happy and together. They have their quiet time in the morning, and they pray. If I could just do it like them, believe it like them, live it like them—I'd be happy, too. I wouldn't be sick.*

But I couldn't do it like them. I couldn't. I felt that I had a lead covering over my heart. And if I could just assault that lead covering, I could feel the right feelings. Most of the time, I didn't know why I had that lead. Now I've got some understanding of why that lead is there, and I think that it is starting to melt off. But it's very, very slow.

Some people are upset that I have to take anti-depressants in order to control my emotional behavior. And sometimes it upsets me, too. When the medication has been working, I'm tempted to think that I don't need it, my condition has improved. A couple of times I've quit taking the pills. But if I don't take them for a week, I end up in the hospital, depressed and suicidal. Once I had to be hospitalized for a month after discontinuing my medication, and last month I was in the hospital for a week.

I guess I still think that if I had faith, I wouldn't have to take the drugs. But my psychiatrist says, "I think it's the *devil* that makes you quit taking your lithium!" And that's probably closer to the truth. Because I know that if I don't take it, I might very well die. Well, if I was diabetic I would take my insulin. I need to keep thinking of it in those terms.

What about the future?

I have no plans for the future. I don't *see* a future. If I do think a year ahead, I see myself right here, in this house, working at the same job, doing everything exactly as I'm doing it now.

I have always been so sure that I was going to die. And I still think I'll be dead by the time I'm thirty-five. I know that when I'm depressed I'm suicidal and I will indeed kill myself if someone doesn't stop me. Realistically speaking, I think it's very likely that one day I'll try to kill myself and there won't be anyone there to stop me. I don't want to struggle all the time, be on drugs all the time. I think I'll run out of things to give to other people, and this is the basis for the work I do and the friendships I have. And when I can't give any more, then what?

So I don't see a future. You've got to remember that I was hospitalized last month, and I've been depressed for three weeks now. I'm only starting to come out of that. Maybe in a couple of weeks I'll have some sense of a personal future. But not now. When I get up in the morning, I tell myself, I'm not going to die today. Whatever this day brings, I'll be able to manage it. Just today. If I go any further into the future than that, I get overwhelmed.

How Low Can You Go?

How strange that I should read this headline today in the morning paper: "Nobody Knows Why Baby Boomers Blue." Apparently my generation, the post-World War II baby boomers, is more depressed than normal.

The reason? The experts confirm my suspicions of the last seven years, verbalizing my thoughts exactly. It seems that along with the major changes in the social environment that have occurred in the past forty years, baby boomers are dealing with "the stress of high expectations clashing with economic reality," according to Robert Hirschfield of the National Institute of Mental Health. The boomers grew up with high expectations for material success, because they grew up in prosperous times. But because they're such a big generation, they find tough competition for each piece of the American Pie. They're having to settle for lower wages, underemployment and unemployment, and less upward mobility than they'd imagined for themselves.

And I know something that isn't mentioned in the article. Christian women, on top of everything else, are having to resolve theologies of entitlement and victory while they're working through weighty personal disappointment. As Carla wondered, "Can I still be a Christian even though I have these problems?"

We're also a psychologically aware generation, states sociologist Allan Horwitz of Rutgers University. We're attuned to look within ourselves and may be more prone to react to difficulties by becoming depressed. Under similar circumstances our parents might have gotten physically sick; we become psychologically ill.

Most of the women I talked to had experience with depression. As a matter of fact, there were only a few who could say that they'd never been more than merely "down" occasionally. The rest spoke of uncontrollable crying, suicide temptations and attempted suicides, spiritual despair, physical deterioration, and feelings of helplessness. Sometimes it lasted for a day or two; sometimes for weeks on end. Some of these women are chronically depressed and many have been hospitalized. Some are fighting it every day; others have more or less succumbed.

Kristine: If I had been forced to be out with people or forced into having people come into my home during those early years with the children, I wouldn't have become depressed. It could have been a really wonderful period in my life if I'd had more friends.

If a woman who is at home with her children is depressed, I think the possibility that she is simply lonesome should be taken very, very seriously.

Shirley: I struggled with suicidal depression before I met the Lord. That was eighteen years ago. I still tend to get "down." When I do, I write to the Lord. I just write my thoughts and feelings and prayers in a notebook. And I say, "God, I know I'm down. And when so-and-so did this today, that really hurt me. You know what?" And I keep writing about the hurt, or the anger. It all comes out on paper, and as I write I can see what's going on with me. It helps me identify the problems and get to the root of what's happening.

This way, the feelings don't stay with me as those vague, depressing thoughts. They're out in the open, where I can deal with them. It really helps me, and now I don't struggle with depression as some people do.

Monica: Moneywise, we just couldn't make it unless I worked. But I just hated leaving my babies! I was raised that the mother was at home, available for her children. It really bothered me that I was working, and I began to feel inadequate as a mother. And then I started feeling inadequate all the way around. I couldn't keep up, as a mom who does everything at home, as a woman working full-time . . . The feelings of guilt and of failure were very strong.

I can see that I was suffering from PMS, and that was making things worse. Also, after my second child was born, I had a severe post-partum depression. But I didn't know any of this at the time. At the time, I only knew that I was being a terrible mother.

I wanted so badly to just send that second child back to wherever she came from. I didn't like her. But then I'd think, *Good mothers don't feel that way about their children.* More guilt. Well, one day I got so angry that I thought I was totally losing control. I became very worried about myself. So I went to work, and talked to one of the doctors at the hospital and said, "I just can't cope any more. I can't do it any more."

He said, "We're going to get you off this merry-go-round. You've got too much to do." He pulled me out of the world, and set me in a mental hospital.

I didn't have to cook anything for anybody, I didn't have to show up for anything, I was able to rest, probably for the first time in eons. I got to thinking that this was the green pasture that the Lord had put me in.

I started to see parts of myself slipping away. And I began to realize how easy it would be to just . . . go. To leave that two-year-old, and leave my responsibilities, and not have to go back to that difficult situation.

One day, I was walking by a mirror, and I looked at myself, and it was the strangest thing: I was empty. There was an empty look in my eyes. And I realized that I had a choice to make. I could stay there at the hospital, I could do puzzles all day, eat the meals they cooked, sit in a rocking chair and look out the window. It's quite a life! And this sounds silly, but as I thought about all this I realized that a life like that would probably drive me crazy. I started to laugh, and that's when I looked in the mirror again and saw that there was still some life left in me.

I also realized that God had not left me. I left the hospital shortly after that—it didn't turn out to be a very long stay. I went home, took a leave of absence from my job, and spent the summer looking after my kids.

When I got home, I became quite introverted because I thought I had failed. I struggled with the belief that Christians shouldn't end up in a mental hospital. A good Christian girl just would not get so far down. So I struggled with guilt: If I'm really a Christian, then why is this happening to me?

Once I accepted Christ as my *personal* Savior, I no longer visualized God as someone in the sky who looked *down* on me, critical of my life and the way I behaved. He became someone who understood, who walked beside me. The burden was definitely lifted, the burden of guilt.

Lee: When I feel really down, I read the Prophets—Jeremiah, death, destruction, desolation. Things don't look so awful in my life after that.

For several years, I went down in the basement and cried in the dark. I thought a lot about Gethsemane. And I thought about how disappointed Christ must have felt when his disciples fell asleep when he was praying because I felt the same sort of abandonment. My husband had fallen asleep during a discussion that was important to me.

Going into the dark basement to cry was, for me, an acting out of death and resurrection. It was my Sheol. And when I came back up, I felt reborn.

The concept of death and resurrection is very central in my thinking, and it's very helpful when I get depressed. Life is a series of deaths and resurrections. I've been in situations where I thought, *This is it, I can't take it any more.* Suicide has often been a temptation for me. But God does lift me up, and I live again. Life is different afterward because it's as if I've died to certain things in my life; but the re-creation that follows is the hope I have.

CIRCUMSTANCES BEYOND OUR CONTROL

Carmen is a friend of mine, a woman who has my respect and affection. She shares some of the wisdom that has come with physical disability.

I had polio when I was a baby. Because of my illness, and because of the disability that came with it, I learned very early on, and my family learned very early on, that you don't necessarily get what you pray for. And that's not the point.

I don't expect a lot. Perhaps I could do with some higher expectations. But I don't expect a lot of things to happen for me. Perhaps I could accomplish more if my expectations were a little higher. Maybe I'm cheating myself out of something that would be fulfilling and something that God wants me to do by being so content with what I have.

I do expect tragedy. I don't take good times for granted. I see good marriages, productive people, happy children . . . I realize that these can end at any moment.

I've had three very close friends die recently. I know that this happens. I know that life is very temporary.

I find myself looking at a family scene—maybe my nieces or nephews—and I *know* and I *think about* the fact that they could die tomorrow. They could get hit by a car. They could come down with leukemia or AIDS or some deadly disease. I know this is true for them because it was true for me.

I do have a sense of the preciousness of life. I do know that it allows me to cherish good times in a way that I might not cherish them if I hadn't experienced tragedy for myself.

When I meet up with someone who has gone through some tragedy, or who lives with some heartache, I am prepared to pity them; lately, however, I find that I experience feelings of jealousy. I am jealous of what they have learned and who they have become in their suffering.

I want to know what Carmen knows—although I am convinced that I can only understand in part what she knows completely. I believe that life is tenuous and precious, as she does. But I haven't lived her life. She has a depth I don't have.

Yet, as we strive to share our experiences, we bestow on each other the gift of our experience and insight. This is very important and very worthwhile.

As you read Bonnie's story you may envy the depth of feeling, the richness of emotion, the quality of love that has come to her through the experience of giving birth to a daughter with spina bifida.

BONNIE'S STORY

Life wasn't easy for Bonnie even before she gave birth to Laurie. She herself suffers from a chronic infection that affects her internal organs, and she has three older children to raise. Amazingly, she finds happiness and comfort in the middle of pain and turmoil.

When I was pregnant, I had two vivid dreams about my baby being hydrocephalic. I shared them with Todd, but of course he didn't experience the dream so he wanted to just brush it off.

When Laurie was born with spina bifida, I had a sense of relief. It was a total shock for Todd—to see her back wide open, and the spine exposed. He couldn't take it.

Our hardest time of adjustment was when she was born. I'm a Lamaze instructor, and I know a lot of statistics about birth defects, and what it does to a family. I know it increases the likelihood of divorce, and I know it's usually the dad who walks out. I couldn't help thinking, *I've got four kids, and one of them is disabled. What if he leaves?*

That thought never entered Todd's mind; he would never walk out on us. But I'm not sure I was totally confident on that point. I had fear.

Right after Laurie's birth, I was hungry for literature and opinions about spina bifida. I read everything I could get my hands on, I talked to everybody. I'd come across something helpful and would shove it in Todd's face, saying, "Read this! Read this!"

He would have none of it. He wanted to go into a closet and shut the door. He denied that it had happened. He thought that if he denied it, then one day she'd just become well.

So here I am: "Read this! Read this!"

And here's Todd: "Be quiet. Leave me alone!"

We ended up fighting. Neither of us is the kind to pout or sulk or hold in our feelings. We fought. And who needs fighting when you're having to spend all your time at the hospital, when you've got decisions to make?

There is one time that stands out in my mind: Laurie was in the hospital, getting ready to have surgery. I went in early in the morning to nurse her, and then came back home to pick up Todd so we could go back to the hospital together. But when I got home, he wasn't there. He was picking up his sister, way over on the other side of town. By the time we finally got hooked up and back to the hospital, they had taken Laurie into surgery. All I could think was, *What if she dies during this operation? What if I never see her alive again? I didn't get to see her that one last time. I didn't get to say good-bye.*

I really laid into Todd—right there in the hospital corridor, with people listening to us. And while I was doing it, I was wondering, *Why am I doing this? She's his daughter, too—he loves her as much as I do. He feels horrible that he missed seeing her before surgery.* But still I was yelling at him in the middle of the hallway. I couldn't stop myself, the emotions were so strong.

After we yelled, we talked. And he realized that some things were very important—such as being there before surgery—and some things weren't—such as picking up his sister, who could have taken a cab to the hospital. At least there was communication!

That's the way it was, and that's the way it is. There are calm times, but then, inevitably, there comes some new crisis, some new decision to make, and we'll be fighting. There are a lot of medical decisions to be made. This puts a lot of pressure on us to think through what we want for Laurie. What responsibilities do we want to take? Her last three surgeries have been optional, but we knew that if she didn't have them, she'd go downhill. Her walking would be harder, her spine would become more deformed. The responsibility is quite a weight.

Todd and I make decisions differently. I want a second opinion, and a third, and a fourth before we decide on an operation. I want to fly her around the country visiting experts. I call the national spina bifida organization and get information on what's the best and latest treatment. Todd's more content to do what our local doctor suggests. It's very hard for us to come to a consensus sometimes.

Our marriage has been pretty solid, but it's always a strain.

ASSUMPTIONS OF HEALTH

I certainly had an assumption that I would be healthy in my adult life because I had been a healthy child. But when I was in college, I contracted a disease that went undiagnosed for over fifteen years.

I cried out for help, to my doctor, to my parents. Either they didn't take me seriously, or they just didn't hear me. I wanted to drop out of college, come home. But my parents wouldn't let me. My doctor's answer was to medicate me. At one point I was taking ten different medications. I was a zombie. I passed out once while driving down the middle of the interstate. Yet, when I told my parents I was afraid to drive, they couldn't seem to understand or accept it. I've had to give that pain to the Lord because I can't deal with it myself.

There was no diagnosis for my disease at that time, so there was no admission that I *had* a disease. For years, I kept my bad health a secret. I couldn't tell anybody what was wrong with me, because I really didn't know.

Finally, I went to a doctor who said, "You have some kind of disease. We just don't know what it is . . . yet." I wanted to hug him. It was the first time that anybody had confirmed what I already knew to be true. He validated what I felt in my own body.

When Laurie was born, we then realized that our lives would never be "easy" again.

She's five now. She's starting to understand the disability, and she's asking questions. Yesterday was a bad day for us, in terms of her bathroom care, and she kept asking me why God made her this way. She said she wanted to be normal.

It's hard to watch that with a child. Yet, if I get depressed, I'm no good to her. I do cry with her—I think that's important. We can cry together. But if I get immobilized by depression, then she's only going to be worse. I simply will not allow myself to go into severe depression.

When I feel it coming on, I run! I'll turn on Christian music or read a book that is very pleasant and uplifting. I take a bath. There are days I'll take ten baths. Todd judges how I feel by how many baths I've had that day.

When I'm in a bath, I can close my eyes and pray and listen to music, and think, *This life's not so bad. I'm in my own home, I have a wonderful family, I'm in a nice hot bathtub . . .*

I cry. I cry a lot. It just comes and I couldn't tell anybody what I'm crying about. I don't really know. It makes our family life bizarre at times—the children will come home from school, and I'm crying, and there's nothing they can do about those tears. It's not normal, I know, for kids to come home and see their mom crying because she has so much pain and sadness. I know it will have an impact on their life. Maybe some good could come from it.

My children know that life is tough, that it isn't fair. They're getting that sooner than a lot of kids.

It's so hard when other Christians tell me that if we really pray and believe that Laurie and I could be healed, then God will do it. They look on our situation, and they interpret it as a lack of faith, a lack of trust, or some terrible sin in our lives.

My sisters are this way. There was a time, when Laurie was a baby, that they would go into the bedroom at my parents' house and pray for her healing, and I wasn't invited.

Finally I just had to tell them that if they couldn't accept her the way she is, then they couldn't be a part of her life. They gave her the message that in order for her to be okay in their eyes, she would have to change—God would have to heal her.

I believe that God knew what she was like before *we* did—before she was born—and that he let her be this way. He's got some plan for all of it.

I need to reassure her that God loves her and has created her the way she is for a purpose. He has a reason, whatever that may be. He's not punishing her.

I know that God heals people today; there's absolutely no question in my mind but that this is true. But I also know he isn't going to do anything miraculous about Laurie's body. I don't believe he wants us to be praying about her healing all the time; I think he wants us to be praying about her disability, and wants us to be open to learning what it is that we're supposed to learn, and living our lives to glorify him through it all.

I love her exactly the way she is. I do *not* want her to grow up thinking that she's let us down. It's not her fault. It's nobody's fault. It's just something that has happened, it's just the way she is. Period.

In a way, it's almost easier to relate to non-Christians on this issue, because they don't believe in healing!

If somebody told me, "I could take Laurie away today and bring her back tomorrow with a perfectly normal body," I think I'd have to say no. Changing her disability would change who she is. And I love her as she is.

Somehow, I can accept Laurie's problem and believe that the Lord is in control.

If I *don't* accept it, and if I *don't* believe the Lord is in control . . . I'm going to go bonkers. I'm going to be so mad and angry at God and everyone else that I'm going to have a miserable life. So I refuse to doubt. I don't dwell on things that I can't change.

To pray for an easy life is to tell God that you don't want any life at all. That you don't want to grow. That you don't want to confront new and challenging situations. That you don't want to rely on him.

In order for us to become more Christ-like, we have to grow. We have to suffer, and we have to fail. I think it's not good to pray that these things won't happen to us; they are what life's all about.

I asked Bonnie to read this transcription of her taped interview, to make sure it was correct. She reported back that she and Todd had had a long discussion about the very words I stumbled over: "If somebody told me, 'I could take Laurie away today, and bring her back tomorrow with a perfectly normal body,' I think I'd have to say no."

Todd challenged Bonnie on it. Was that true? She wouldn't accept a new, perfectly normal body for her daughter? After more deliberation her answer was unchanged. She loves Laurie as she is. Period.

CHAPTER EIGHT

Church

*W*hen discussing the subject of the church (whether the local church of membership or the Christian community in general), women talked of the expectations put on them by the church. Even more, however, they described the expectations *they* had for the church: that the church will preach the gospel, provide leadership, set standards of behavior, and demand accountability of the congregation. This is what Christians do for each other; this is what Christians do for the world.

Hurting women look to the church for more. They want comfort in their times of need; they expect to be ministered to when they're going through hard times.

Is the Christian community providing the prophetic voice—the call to repentance and the challenge to the higher life—*more forcefully* than it is actively ministering to those of its membership who are in need? Is it involving itself in the deepest needs of its members? Charles Swindoll claims the church is the only army that shoots its wounded. Is that true?

If so, then we really have no one but ourselves to blame. The church isn't some far-off bureaucracy beyond our influence. *We* are the church. We each have a voice, we each have a part to play, we each contribute something to its character and expression.

It would have been nice to hear more positive things said about churches. What you will read is what I was told when I quizzed women about their churches or Christian support groups. Not much happy talk followed.

Margie relates her disappointment with the church and recalls her own shortcomings within the body.

> My oldest son was raised in a Christian home, raised with high moral ideals. Both my husband and I have been very involved in his life, very in touch with what he's needed along the way. Yet he isn't walking with the Lord. When he was in high school, he got involved in drugs and drinking. Then he married a non-Christian girl—they had to get married. And my youngest son—he doesn't do drugs like the other one, but he's lukewarm. He doesn't follow the Lord.
>
> My husband and I had claimed Proverbs' "Train up a child in the way he should go and he will not depart from it." We believed that if we did all the right things, he would grow up to be a Christian. We also had been praying for a Christian wife for our son ever since we found out that you're "supposed" to do that. I wanted a fairy-tale relationship. I wanted to be Naomi, I wanted her to be Ruth. We were very disappointed, still are.
>
> There was no support in our church. Where were the other parents who were going through this? We felt like the only ones, though we've

since realized that we weren't. We expected the leaders of our church to do more for our son because he was still attending church.

We had given the church our tithe, our service, our devotion—and we fully expected to get something back in our time of need. We thought it would be there for us, but it wasn't. The leaders were pouring their time and efforts into the situations that would bring quick results: the kids who responded positively, right away. But we thought that those kids were going to get turned on to the Lord anyway. Our son really *needed* their help.

We haven't left that church; we continue to support it in every way. But we got no support for our grief. The Bible says, "Weep with those who weep, rejoice with those who rejoice." I had this terrible grief, but no one would weep with me. On the other hand, I was not rejoicing with those who were rejoicing.

I believe that if you've lived through a particular difficulty, it's your responsibility to help others who are going through the same thing. That's one of God's purposes in letting you go through it. I don't think there's enough teaching on this. People say, "Whew, I'm glad that's over." They don't want to open up the wound again; they want to stay in their comfort zone. But we need to realize our responsibility. And in the church, we need to organize for it. We need support groups and counseling and encouragement to share our journey. We need to be available. How about a Sunday school class called "For Hurting Parents"? Parents could attend when they need it.

A friend of mine is going through a very difficult time with her children. A speaker came to their church—a well-respected man, a published author, a leader in the evangelical Christian community. He spoke on self-esteem and said that if the parents are giving children the esteem they need, those kids will turn out all right.

There were wounded families there, families that had real troubled kids. I don't think that kind of teaching has any place in the church. If there were a set of rules that conscientious parents could follow and thereby insure that their kids would turn out all right, well, conscientious parents would follow them to the letter!

But there is no set of rules. I like the illustration that Dr. Dobson used in *Parenting Isn't for Cowards.* He talked about a wedding he had attended. At the end, balloons were released from a box. The balloons were all made out of the same fabric, filled from the same canister of helium. When the balloons were launched, some went high into the sky, some got lodged in the trees, and some bounced around on the ground.

That's the way it is. You fill your kids with the best stuff you can; some kids will soar, and some will get hung up, and some will never leave the ground. Children are not a blank sheet of paper that we write whatever we want on. They are made by God a certain way, and they make their own choices. This isn't taught enough in the churches.

What kind of children did that speaker have?

Great children—all adults, all turned out perfectly. I've known other church leaders who have had the same situation. They raised their kids right, and they turned out right. And none of them can understand or sympathize with parents who raised their kids right, and saw them turn out wrong.

I've had to live down some things I said before I had teenagers. I once said in a women's group: "Well, if you don't want your children to listen to rock music, you just forbid it. It's as simple as that." And on another occasion, when a mother asked what you do if you know your daughter is sexually active (do you counsel her on birth control or not) I said, "If you have raised your daughter right, the question won't even come up. She will not be sexually active." My kids were young. I didn't know what I was talking about.

This woman told me that she said to herself at the time, "I wonder what the Lord is going to bring into Margie's life to help her see how judgmental she's being?" She was too wounded at the time to approach me, but years later, when I was going through all this stuff with my son, she said, "You see now that there are no easy answers."

Now I teach that the Proverbs are principles, not promises. And I get it from the other direction! I have young mothers coming up to me, and they say, "Margie, I disagree with you. Don't teach that. I am claiming God's *promise* that if you train up a child in the way he should go he won't depart from it. I don't want to hear you talk about principles. It is a promise."

Look at Jacob and Esau. Isaac loved one over the other. The children had done nothing good or bad to deserve Isaac's love or rejection; they had made no choices. That's just the way it was, in order to show God's purpose.

It's grief to me, really, it's grief to me. But I must let God be God. Our purpose here on earth is to bring glory to God. And who am I to say how that will be accomplished? It's my deepest desire for my children to walk with the Lord always, but I can't make that happen. I have to let God do his work.

I do a lot of speaking to women's groups, and I always try to find a way to work in that I was divorced, and that I have a son who is not walking with the Lord.

The comment I get more than anything else is, "Thank you for sharing about your divorce, about your son. Because women look up to you, and if *you're* struggling, there's hope for me. Please don't quit sharing that."

I don't like sharing these failures. I don't like digging them up, and I'd really rather have everybody think that I'm a great success at everything I do. But I know it's important. And I get encouragement, too. I've had women come up to me and say, "I was just like your son in high school. Don't give up. I'm a Christian now; perhaps he'll find the Lord, too." This sort of thing can only happen when we start sharing honestly with one another.

When I edit out the painful, confusing, unfinished parts of The Alice Lawhead Story, it sounds good. Darn good. As long as I accentuate the positive and conceal the negative, I can protect myself from criticism and pity. I can also build a big, thick stone wall between myself and everyone I care about.

To tell the *whole* truth requires a balanced testimony. We are charged in Scripture to sing songs of praise, yes, but also to bear one another's burdens.

Margie's experience is my own: When I disclose my failures—in what I write, or what I say—there is a big payoff. I bond to women who have also had pain, and they bond to me. There is trust. Once problems are out in the open, then there is the opportunity to share solutions. I have access to practical advice. I can be encouraged and comforted and prayed for.

WHAT THE CHURCH EXPECTS

Rose: The big emphases in the church I grew up in were evangelism and mission. There were a lot of things a person was expected to do, but basically it boiled down to this: that your mission in life was to be a great one. I expected to be extremely successful spiritually. I would know exactly what to do, and I would do it.

I spent two summers doing mission work with Indians in Oklahoma—a very rural existence, very hard, very dirty. I became convinced that I either wasn't able or wasn't called to live that way.

I felt guilty. In the end, I went with my gut feeling about it, but my head kept saying, *How are you going to reconcile your decision with "Go ye into all the world and preach the gospel"*?

I've always felt a little bit out of step with the Christians I know. They don't support the arts, and that's my life. They say art is cake, and you don't need cake to survive. Of course, when I was growing up in church, they were always glad to have someone who would make posters. . . .

I have struggled with this issue: Am I trying to fit God into my art, or is art what God is calling me to do? My artist friends pursue art for its own sake, but I realize that there has to be a purpose for this. How can I live out God's purpose in my life?

I've given up the idea of aligning myself with other people who are interested in growing and interested in my growth. I just can't seem to find a group like that. I go to church, but I'm an anonymous attender—there's no intimacy. I'm listening to God these days.

The church doesn't seem to be much involved in growth; that's what I heard. So many people talked about the church's expectations in terms of behavior; so few spoke of the church expecting them to mature in their faith.

> **Tricia:** I suppose that I have imagined expectations in the past. At church I've assumed that other people have expectations for me. They think I'll serve on a committee or participate in some activity or take on some responsibility. There is a certain amount of participation that *is* expected when you're a member of a local church body, and I personally agree with that.
>
> I believe that a person sets his own pace in a church and, having set it, expectations will follow. Once they figure out that you're committed, that you're a "doer," then you'll get asked to do things, and it will be expected that you get them done.

> **Emily:** People at church expect me, as a woman, to come up with cakes for their bake sales or to serve on the nursery committee because I've got babies. It's role playing.
>
> And I do those things because I don't mind it too much. I'm not inspired to do it; it doesn't give meaning to my life. It's a duty. It's something I do to be nice.
>
> I distance myself from the other women in my church. I don't want to be a fat, ugly, frumpy church lady. I don't want to wear polyester, I don't like to sit around with other women at church and talk about kids and housecleaning.

I guess I'm proud of being a model. That's a non-boring, undull thing to be. It's even a little racy. If I can remember that I'm an model, then I don't get threatened by baking cookies for Vacation Bible School.

I guess I do care if people at church think I'm not a very good church helper. But I don't lose sleep over it. I'm not on five committees; I don't get up and make speeches, ask people to go to the spaghetti rally. I'm not in the handbell choir. I'm not the warm, fuzzy woman who will do everything all the time.

Melissa: My husband and I don't live up to our church's expectations, I suppose. We drink, for one thing. But we don't feel bad because we just don't share all their convictions and values, and we're comfortable with that.

I think we feel this way partly because we've moved around so much. I have been in a lot of churches, lots of different kinds, and I can't afford to live or die by the fellowship I'm in. I need for my relationship with the Lord to be the kind of relationship that can survive this sort of uprooting. If I'm looking to my church or Bible study group for approval and for their direction in my life—for their "expectations"—then I'm in trouble.

Irene: I remember feeling guilty, guilty, guilty all the time. I wrote to my Young Life leader and told him about it. I was having nightmares a lot—and some for good reason. He sent me the book *Guilt and Grace* by Paul Tournier.

My husband and I went on a camping trip, and I remember sitting on the banks of the river and reading this book. The first half is all about guilt, and as I was reading it I thought, *This isn't exactly what I need. I know all about guilt. When do I get to the grace?*

In the middle of the book, Tournier talks about a friend he had who knew all about him and loved him. One of my Young Life staff friends was like that for me; she knew everything about me, and she loved me. It finally dawned on me that this is possible with God, too. He knows, and he still loves. It turned me around.

THOSE WOMEN'S GROUPS

Judith: I feel pretty well accepted; most of us in the group are in the same boat. We have children, we have some problems, and we feel pretty open about sharing.

There are a couple of people that I don't feel comfortable with when I have certain things to say. I'll say, "Oh, I can't get along with my mother-in-law; I don't want to be with her this weekend," and this other group member will reply, "Well, you shouldn't feel that way." Now, what good does that do? Then I can add guilt to my feelings about my mother-in-law. Denying it isn't going to change it, and I'm not going to deny it so this other woman will feel better.

Darlene: I have felt very strong expectations from my church: to be active in the women's group, to be a stay-at-home mother. To be that perfect wife, the Proverbs 31 lady.

I'm not that way. I'm not the woman who keeps her house clean, is the last one to bed at night and the first one up in the morning.

I didn't want the women in my Bible study group to know that I wasn't fulfilling these roles. But eventually it became too much to keep inside, and I had to share it all with them.

Some of them couldn't accept what I was telling them. I could see it in their faces. They didn't want to hear about my problems and my failures. They seemed to be saying, "Why can't she just cope with it? God has promised in the Bible to give her whatever strength she needs to face her problems. Why can't she just manage these matters?"

I was tempted to say nothing more, to keep quiet about it. But then I thought, *No, this is a chance for them to learn how to empathize a little bit. And if they can't understand it, perhaps they can learn to sympathize.* So I continued to be vocal; I still ask for their prayers.

Not everyone was resistant. Some were wonderful! If I didn't show up for church on a Sunday morning, they'd ask about me, and if Nate told them I wasn't feeling well, they'd be over with a meal for the family. They were active in their support.

There's one woman who is a nurse, and whenever I share that I'm having problems, she's quick with advice. "You should try this," or "Why doesn't your doctor do that." *I'm* learning how to accept her useless advice with a certain amount of grace because I realize that she is well-intentioned, and this is her way of showing that she cares about me. If you're going to ask for prayer, you've got to be willing to accept the advice that's sure to come with it!

Meredith: I keep getting these messages that if I had my priorities straight, my house would be clean and my children would be happy and my husband would be fulfilled. If my priorities were straight, I'd get up early in the morning and have devotions and clean the house and make a cooked breakfast. . . .

For a while, I went to a church Bible study. There was so much pressure! Instead of being a support group, it was a list of all the things we ought to be doing for Christ. I left feeling guilty for all the things I *didn't* do every day. Like hospitality. That's the big thing now—we're supposed to open up our homes daily to other people, to welcome them. I just can't handle it. I don't see how people can do it. I can't entertain; it's too stressful. To get the house neat enough, prepare a meal, and then be bright and funny through dinner—argh! I want to crash at the end of the day, not throw a dinner party.

OKAY, NOW MINISTERS' WIVES SPEAK OUT

The pressures of being a part of the church family may be great. The pressures of being in full-time ministry can be well nigh unbearable sometimes. I know, because I grew up in a parsonage. Want to hear the Slaikeu family saga? Here's my mother speaking:

> There's no doubt but that the worst time in our lives was our first pastorate. For years after we left, I could get sweaty palms just thinking about it.
>
> We were given a twelve-room apartment to live in—in the church! We had stained glass in our bedroom, and several of the rooms had no windows at all. It was heated with soft coal, so there was a cloud of dust all the time, dust that settled on the furniture and in our hair. People in the church felt free to walk in without knocking, to pull up a chair at any meal, to sit and watch me while I nursed the babies. There was no yard for the children to play in; I had to ask our neighbor's permission to put Karl's playpen in her yard, on the other side of the alley. No privacy whatsoever.

I wasn't born yet. But this was how my three older brothers spent their early years. And that wasn't even the worst of it:

> The church was run by a very powerful man who wasn't even a member of the church—his wife was. He was the head usher, he was on the Board of Trustees, he set the agenda for the whole church. Arthur had to fight that man all the time—and it wasn't easy. When we couldn't live in the church any more—we needed to get a house—they couldn't get a loan for the parsonage from any bank in town because this man had told all of the bankers that if they loaned money to the church, he'd personally see to it that the mortgage wasn't repaid. He controlled the business interests of many church members because he personally held their mortgages or business loans that they'd taken out. He was forever laying down ultimatums about how the church was run, how its affairs were controlled.
>
> I ran across a letter a few years back from Arthur to this man. It was written when we left the church. And it was an apology. Arthur said he regretted that he had spent so much time fighting him, and so little time working to win him to the Lord.

When you live in a parsonage (or twelve-room apartment in the church, as the case may be), you learn to take the good with the bad. Along with the reassuring sense of being immersed in full-time ministry, there are the day-to-day obstacles to confront and overcome:

> **Marsha:** The hardest thing about being married to a minister is his absence. When my husband was a student, he was home; I was the one

who was away, and he was always at home and available. But now he's gone all day and gone many nights of the week with meetings and calling. I wish there was some way that I could help him, free up some of his time so that he could share more in Stephanie's and my day.

Sydney: If you're a pastor's wife, there are so many things you can't share with your friends. A lot of what you hear and know is confidential, and you don't want people to think that you're just generally dispersing information. It's good to have a reputation of being discreet.

Because it isn't good for either one of us to talk a lot with our friends, Curt and I have become closer since he entered the ministry. We can talk to each other.

And when we are with a minister from another church, we feel that we can be pretty open about our feelings—especially as they relate to what's going on in church.

If the choice was mine, I wouldn't want to be in ministry. We live under pressure all of the time, constantly aware of other people's needs and knowing that we're here to minister to those many, many needs.

It would be so nice to come to church like everybody else and sit together in the pew, and just be. Just worship. Not to worry about when the service is going to get over, or if the piano is tuned, or if so-and-so's needs are being met, or if that old man will finally die this week. All these concerns lay on our shoulders and I get so tired of it. Morning, noon and night; weekends and holidays. It never eases up.

Dorcas: The church came first in Harry's life. He admitted this, but he felt that I was his partner. Even our children were in partnership with

him, and it was an exciting life with lots to do and
great rewards and importance.

He did the work of the church and my
participation in ministry was to keep house and
watch the children so that he was free to work.
After church, there would be youth fellowship,
and other get-togethers. He'd go to them, and
I'd go home and get the children in bed. I'd get a
little depressed.

Cindy: I rebel against the idea that, as a
pastor's wife, I should come under closer scrutiny
than any other Christian. It's my belief that the
priesthood of the believer makes you just as accountable as I am.

The wife of the minister who held this post
before Adrian did blazed a lot of ground, and I'm
thankful to her for that. She accustomed the
congregation to the fact that ministers' wives
have lives of their own and callings of their own.
She did a lot of educating, and I am the benefi-
ciary of her courage.

As a mother, most of my support comes from
Adrian—I wouldn't want to have a child with any
other man for a husband. After that, I think the
most support comes from a neighbor who lives
two doors down. We watch each other's children,
and when the weather is nice, we take long walks
together. I feel that she shares many of my values,
especially family values.

**What is it about her that's most helpful?
That she'll watch your daughter for you?**

No, it's that she doesn't go to my church. I
feel free to say what's on my mind around her,
because there's no way it'll get around to the
congregation. As a pastor's wife, that means a lot
to me: to have someone outside my immediate
Christian community that I can share with.

Theresa: Here I am, a woman minister of an evangelical congregation. Yet I feel that I have the status that a black person had about a hundred years ago. In a group of pastors, I am ignored. What I say isn't taken seriously. My church is expected to fail, not to grow.

I had very good role models with the nuns who taught me in school. Nuns are very independent women, highly educated, invested in careers in the church. They were my models. They never made me feel as though I was second-class because I was a girl.

A lot of women tell me that they have no women to follow, no women leaders. I see myself sponsoring other women into ministry, I see them growing under my tutelage. I expect continued discrimination and adversity from men who cannot accept my calling, but I also see my church growing and some change of attitude from some people.

"THERE NEEDS TO BE A PLACE FOR HEALING"

Monica: When I started having problems with my teenagers, I started sharing in small groups, and that's when I finally realized how hurting people are underneath their happy faces.

I felt that everyone else had it all together and that there was something terribly wrong with me. I couldn't keep up. The church's standards, not God's, made me feel guilty. Luckily, we're getting away from this—at least in my church. There is *so* much hurt, so much turmoil, that people are beginning to give up on presenting a brave front to the rest of the congregation.

I believe that the minister of a church sets the tone for the degree of openness in that church. For example, our new associate minister has told the congregation from the pulpit that he is a recovering alcoholic. This goes a long way in encouraging members of the congregation to be more open with each other about their own personal struggles.

I started a support group in our church for parents who have problems with their teenagers; it came out of a prayer group I was in. As we were sharing prayer requests and praying for each other I was sharing about my problems with my son. Another woman in that group then shared her concerns, and we started a support group from that. It takes a little patience at the beginning, because people are reluctant to share everything.

Even if there isn't a whole lot of honesty in the Sunday morning service amongst all members of the church, there can at least be some degree of openness among some members of the congregation. There needs to be a way to say, "If you're having a problem, we can talk about it." What we've got to *quit* saying is that these problems don't happen in the church. Because they do, and they happen to the best of families. Instead of covering up the sin, it needs to be more exposed so that people can come and say, "I've really got a problem in this area, and I need help."

Cheryl: The last time Brad beat me up, I went over to the house of our pastor and his wife the next morning. They had been counseling us. She saw the blood, she saw where my earring had been ripped out of my ear.

She knew what was going on, but when I said I was going to get a divorce, all support dropped away. My pastor asked me if I had "scriptural grounds for divorce." Brad wasn't adulterous so when I heard my pastor say those words, I felt that I would be locked into that marriage for life. I couldn't handle it. It was the worst thing that man could have said to me.

I'm not saying divorce is right. I believe that God cares about people being whole. I believe that we need to break the "laws" sometimes in order for that to happen. I believe the highest law is love. When you have two people tearing each other apart, when there's abuse . . .

I would never advocate divorce; I would never recommend it to someone else. But I can tell you that *not once* have I regretted my divorce. Not once. When I was married to Brad, I was enabling him to be a jerk. I wasn't strong—I wasn't strong enough to stand up to him without getting my brains beat out. There's no way I know of that it could have worked out under those circumstances, no way. And that's okay. I accept responsibility for what I did.

I did it for my kids, too. Brad treated them the same way he treated me. I had to get them out of that situation, or they would have been saddled with even more baggage to carry with them through their adult lives. They would have had a horrible concept of God if they were thinking that their own father was like God. Brad used God to support everything he did, every rotten thing.

When it became clear to my church that I was going to go ahead and go through with a divorce, they kicked me out of everything I was involved in. All my leadership responsibilities were taken away.

I can understand that there needs to be a place for healing, and that it can be a good thing to give a person like me some space, and that I may not have been fit for leadership at that time. I also admit that I was getting a lot of my identity as a person and as a Christian from the things I was *doing*, which was not the best way to get that identity. On the other hand, to have all those things taken away from me at a time when I needed support and acceptance was very hard. The bottom fell out.

When I came to this city to this job, there were no questions asked. People didn't quiz me about my divorce, about whether or not it was "scriptural." They took me in, they offered help, they loved me, prayed with me, supported me, gave me friendship. The divorce was never a wall between us. They've been God's arms.

CLAIRE'S STORY

Claire's story is one of abandonment, abuse, drugs, eating disorders—and healing. Her own experiences have led her to work in a clinical setting with anorexics and bulimics, developing effective means of treating compulsive behavior.

One night, when I was eight years old, my father was out of town on a business trip. My mother handed me a dollar and said, "Here, you babysit your brothers and sisters." She left and never came back home.

I didn't have many "normal" childhood experiences after that. I did all the cooking and cleaning and looking after the younger children. I did the grocery shopping and took the children to school in the morning. When we were living in a duplex, I got paid for raking leaves and for cleaning the laundry room.

The only activities I remember were church-related: Sunday school, church, evening church, choir, bell choir, Friday night socials.

By the time I was a teenager, I knew that I didn't want to be a wife and mother. I'd already taken care of a house of children. That role wasn't okay; there wasn't a lot of gratification with that. I never envisioned leaving home, finding a husband, falling in love, getting married, having babies and living happily ever after.

When I was in high school, my father remarried. This woman used to come into my room at night, read the Bible to me, and tell me that my mother was a whore and that she was going to hell. So I ran away from home to my mother's house. I showed up on her doorstep, having had no previous relationship with her. People had given me bits and pieces of my mother, and I needed to know her for myself, to find out what was true and what wasn't.

A court battle came out of this: My father accused my mother of kidnaping me. A minister that I had seen through my father's church testified in court on behalf of my father, really twisting things I had said to him. So I stood up in court and called him a liar. I knew that I'd turned a corner then, because you just don't stand up in court and call your minister a liar. As it turned out, I was returned to my father and stepmother. But I realized that I would have to live life on my own.

This was in the sixties, and I was in California. I was very much a child of the sixties; I got involved in what you would expect: the counterculture, drugs. I did a lot of hallucinogenic drugs and had a lot of crazy experiences. But to this day, as bizarre as it sounds and as hard as it might be to believe, when I was doing drugs I experienced God for the first time. I felt the presence of God, and it was a very comforting thing. The message I got was that I was okay and that I was part of a bigger plan. What I was learning would be tools that I would use later.

Secretly, I went out and bought the first version of the Good News Bible that had come out. In reading Scripture, I learned something very different from what I had been taught in church, which was hellfire and damnation, guilt, misery, separation from the world.

I was anxious to learn, and to figure out how I fit into the world. So I took training in a number of faiths. I went through the whole Catholic catechism, I went through Mormon indoctrination, attended an Episcopal church, and got involved with Jehovah's Witnesses. I went to the Hare Krishnas, too, and felt that at least there was a sense of love and acceptance there that I wasn't finding elsewhere. I wasn't really looking in the right places. There was no way to get a sense of "self" in these religions. In their own ways, they were all built on works, not faith.

Meanwhile, I was doing well in school, getting good grades and taking part in student government, but my family life was getting worse and worse. My father became reclusive, and my stepmother became alcoholic and physically violent. By the time I was seventeen, I knew that I couldn't stay there anymore. I ran away to Haight-Ashbury on the back of a motorcycle.

I learned a lot about values, about the world. I became active in Vietnam protests, got involved with street people. I did come back home in my senior year of high school. By this time my stepmother was extremely violent. I had to go to school with black eyes and bruises. A retired police officer I knew realized that things were really bad for me; he helped me find an apartment with another girl who was in a similar situation, so I moved away from home for the last time. I dropped out of high school.

I met a man who was even needier than I was. We had a relationship, I got pregnant, we married. I had my first child when I was eighteen. I wanted that child very badly; pregnancy was an ecstatic time for me. I couldn't have cared less about the marriage, but the baby was important.

EATING DISORDERS

I developed anorexia nervosa when I was thirteen; I couldn't maintain that, so I became bulimic until I was twenty-two. This was during a time when people didn't even know much about alcoholism—*nobody* knew anything about eating disorders. There was no place to talk about it or even any recognition that anything was wrong.

You were anorexic, then bulimic. What happened?

It came at a time when I was totally engrossed in Scripture, and I had a heightened spiritual awareness. I began *feeling* things for the first time: anger, hurt, resentment. The purging became a symbolic act of recognition of those feelings.

Bulimia was the first step to unfreezing the emotions that I hadn't been able to deal with. It was a step toward wholeness.

My spiritual journey . . . I discovered such a difference between the sayings of Jesus and what my church taught. His emphasis on love, on faith and grace, not works. I couldn't figure out how the church could be the way it was, if the Bible was the way *it* was. As I grew up in the church, going to Sunday school, even accepting Christ as my personal Savior, I never had a sense of love or a sense of understanding or peace. The important things were attendance, tithing, and whether or not you remembered your Bible or studied the Sunday school lesson. Everybody said, "You're going to feel something very different," but I never did.

I know it sounds terrible to link up my realization of God's love for me with my experiences with drugs, but that *did* happen. I figure that God is going to get through to us however he can. And if that's what was necessary with me, well, I'm real grateful. I began to understand that there was a loving God who cared about me, who was not going to let me down, and who I could have with me wherever I went and whoever I was with.

I hit a crossroad with the birth of my second child; I was twenty-one. I was still practicing bulimia at that time, and through the pregnancy I binged and purged and used laxatives. She was born with physical deformities, and the medical personnel said that she would be profoundly retarded. Although I took full responsibility for her condition, I was angry with God, too.

I took my daughter home from the hospital, against the advice of the social workers. She didn't respond to me at all, didn't cry, didn't move, didn't do anything you would expect. I became so profoundly depressed that I attempted suicide. Through the subsequent hospitalization, I got a dose of reality therapy from a nurse in the hospital, who told me that I had responsibilities, and I had tools that God had given me that would help me carry on those responsibilities. And I'd better do it.

I thought, *How dare you? It's God who has let down on his responsibilities.* But God wasn't saying to me, "I want you to throw up three times a day and take a hundred laxatives a day." He was saying, "You must take care of the body you have been given. It's your responsibility."

I started going to church. We met in a tent on Sundays and in homes during the week. It was a very family-oriented ministry, and I got my first understanding of what church really is. I got a realistic understanding of Scripture. The church was very charismatic—there were healings and tongues and the charismatic gifts. It was very real to me, and I never doubted any of it.

I started healing.

How far into the future do you look?

Just today. I know that each day will provide me with at least one challenge and one opportunity. I try very hard to look for the blessings in my day; I do that very consciously during my drive to work. The people I meet by chance, or the people I'm scheduled to see or whatever . . . I know that I will have an opportunity to share, and an opportunity to learn. Everything I experience will be okay.

That shows a lot of confidence.

I feel like I've got a lot of confidence. I don't know what I would be given that I couldn't get through. If I carry one fear, it's the death of my husband—or the death of a child. But if I spend my life being focused on my fears, I can't do much.

It is because you've been through so much, and you're here to tell about it?

No, it's because I've been on an inner journey with God. I've spent a lot of years looking inside. I've found a lot of things I like, and a lot of things I don't like. I've learned there are ways to deal with what I don't like, and it is my responsibility to do that.

Throughout the journey, I have seen too many blessings and gifts. I can take them, leave them, stumble over them, or ignore them. But they're there. I decide what to do about it. My job is to keep walking, to keep the process going, to take care of myself, to keep working on my understanding.

I know I'm not going to get it all right, but I'm satisfied with the pieces I'm getting right. That's okay.

The daughter who was born with physical and mental handicaps is now a teenager and, after years of medical attention and special care, is quite normal—the joy of her mother's life.

CHAPTER NINE

Doing and Being

Angela: I was in high school, and I'd won some kind of award or something—anyway, something neat had come my way. And my mother said, "Enjoy it while you can, because you'll be mediocre in the end."

When I was a teenager, I thought that once I had finished school, gotten a job, entered the adult world, and walked down the aisle in my own wedding, life became a glide into obscurity. At that time, it wouldn't have surprised me at all to hear a mother say that life became mediocre in the end; it's what I believed myself.

Yet, now that I'm entering middle age, I cringe at such words. More, I'm terrified of them. Is it true? Does life become mediocre in the end?

Some women I talked to had believed that nothing special would come to them in their lives. They were either confirmed in this belief or found themselves surprised by how interesting and fulfilling their lives became. Others expected great and wonderful things; if they weren't getting those wonderful things, they wondered why. "Why haven't I turned out to be something special? After all, I was a cheerleader. I was class president and valedictorian. I was a National Merit scholar. I dated the cutest boys. I had so much going for me."

Doing and being: How much of my identity is caught up in my accomplishments, my physical attributes, my capabilities and possessions? What happens when I discover limitations, experience failures, confront poverty?

PERFECT IS AS PERFECT DOES

Elizabeth: I have the kind of perfectionism that's a sickness. How can I even begin to reach my goals with this kind of flaw [a divorce] on my record?

I was born with a competitiveness that has served me well and done me in. In work, I've been competitive; I've tried to do my absolute best. And that doesn't hurt anybody; everybody wins when that happens. On the other hand, I've been competitive in relationships, and it's been totally inappropriate and has damaged me and other people. Relationships aren't the place to compete.

This competitiveness comes from the need to quantify my self-worth. To show that I do have value as a person, through winning, improving, doing things better than others.

I can't be happy unless I know I'm doing the best I can, that I'm being the best I can be. But sometimes my best is . . . it's kind of bad.

Can you live with that?

I *want* to be able to live with that. Because it will mean that my standards are more internal, more valid for me. It will mean that I've given up comparing myself with everybody else, competing with certain people and measuring myself against arbitrary standards.

Suzanne: It bothers me that I'm such a perfectionist. And when I don't attain perfection, I'm very difficult to live with, because I'm so angry at myself. I suspect that I'll never get over this completely, although I can hope to improve. My standards for myself are so much higher than other people's standards for me. I don't have to sit around and wait for others to tell me I'm screwing up. I know it long before anybody else does.

Fay: I've had to learn to let go of some of my perfectionism. In college, I had to have top grades. My dorm room had to be neat and clean. I'd give 100 percent at work. But I just can't do that anymore, and I'm coming to the point where I don't blame myself for it.

I had to learn this by degrees. When our daughter was born, I would get her to bed at night, and then I'd do whatever work I hadn't been able to get done during the day. Maybe I'd start at 11:00, and work until 3:00 A.M. This wasn't uncommon. And I had a meticulous house. Everything was perfect. Raymond and I were church youth leaders when she was a baby, and I was discipling a girl who came over a lot during the week. I thought that I needed to do all these things.

Now I don't think that way. It wasn't an overnight realization, an identifiable turning point. I credit Raymond with helping me see the light. He's my personality opposite, very relaxed and laid back.

Perhaps the biggest thing was that my father died during this time. Going through his illness and death helped me see what was important and what wasn't. I began to see that time is precious, and you have to establish priorities about your time. Seeing him die, and knowing that I will die one day, had a profound effect on me.

Life is short, and it's precious. I don't feel the need anymore to get so shook up about little things. A clean house is not so important in the big scheme of things.

Linda: For a long time, I wasn't sure what my limitations were. I didn't know what I could be, what I couldn't be, or how everything would fit together. But now I don't feel guilty about my limitations; I can live with them.

STRIVING TOWARD THE GOAL

Because I'm goal-oriented, I have always been intrigued by people who don't set goals. Of course, I can see that goal-setting can be self-serving and can run counter to what God intends for us to do. If I believe that God has a plan for my life, how can I reconcile that with the goals I set for myself every day? If I am in tune with God's will, will my goals naturally work toward his plan? Are my goals themselves part of his plan? What about when I don't reach my goals—does that mean that I've failed to fulfill his plan? Or that my goals were outside his will in the first place?

I never realized how "American" goal-setting was until I lived in Britain. In the church we attended, we sang a song that had as part of its refrain, "Do not strive, do not strive." I couldn't quite understand this. I had always resonated with Paul's admonition to keep striving toward the goal. Keep working, keep planning, keep moving ahead, keep going for the gold. A woman in my Bible study group said, "I don't believe that I have ever consciously set my sights on anything with the intention of getting it." Another woman who did a considerable amount of counseling said that she found, in her practice, that striving was at the root of many of her clients' problems.

Sometimes I don't think I could get out of the bed in the morning without defining it as a goal to do so. Every day I make a list of the things I will do that day, and each item on the list is a goal. I make goals for my family. I had it as a goal that Ross would quit dragging a bottle of juice around the house by the time he was two. I planned for Drake to be totally toilet trained by the age of three. When I write a book, the deadline agreed to by me and the publisher is my goal, and I pride myself in meeting these deadlines. My diet, exercise program (such as it is), socializing are all expressed as goals. I rarely go for a walk; I go for a walk for a certain distance, to be covered within a specific time. I do not meander aimlessly around the neighborhood; I have a destination.

Therefore I have been very intrigued and challenged by the following women, who do not approach their lives as one long, endless string of goals.

Ingrid: I don't understand why women set themselves up with these high expectations. I always thought that once you grew up, you got past the dreams and expectations. Yet I have friends my age, and they're still going through this! They're setting themselves up, and they're passing it all along to their children—the unrealistic expectations for life.

I wonder if they realize that ten years from now they're going to be *so* disappointed. Their kids aren't going to live up to all these dreams;

they won't continue to dress in the cute little clothes, do all the cute little things. Life is a daily thing. I don't understand people who live in a dream world.

My husband and I have this joke; we always talk about when we're rich and famous. With four kids, I can't see that we'll ever be rich; and we're not going in the direction of fame at all. So it's a joke. But we have friends who do think in those terms, seriously. A friend of ours was talking to my husband the other day, saying things like, "I'm not providing for my wife," and "By this point in my life I thought I'd be . . . I'd have this much money, I'd be this well known, I'd have accomplished these things. But I haven't done all those things. I'm still back here in the same old house with the same wife and working at the same job."

But my husband said, "Look, I grew up in the Midwest. Everyone in my family worked hard all their lives at their jobs. They had used furniture. They retired, and they didn't have anything except Social Security to retire on. It was never expected that it would be any different than that." And who's to say it will be different for us? Who's to say we'll ever have new furniture or big savings or an exciting life? We're going to work, and we're going to see our children get married and leave home, and we're going to retire with the same furniture we have now. We may never go to Europe.

Yet most of our friends—and most of them are Christians—still have these big dreams of financial success, travel, fame. At what point can they say, "This is what I've got now. Lord, thanks for what I've got; show me how to be wise with what I have and with what you have for me."?

When I'm with people who are so dissatisfied, I just want to say, "Grow up. Be satisfied with what you have. It may never change. Why invest so much energy in dreams? Put your energy into what you have now. Enjoy it. Quit worrying about the future."

I know a lot of this is just personality differences, so I don't say what I'd like to say. I keep my mouth shut. But still, I can't understand it.

Karen: I've never been goal-oriented. It's not like me to sit around and dream about what I'd like to be someday: a mommy or a librarian or a doctor. I've just taken life as it came.

Every now and then I take stock of my situation: what Bob is doing, where the kids are developmentally and in school, what their interests are and what mine are. And I see what I can do within that framework. It changes constantly. But that's workable for me, not to set goals far in advance for things that I want to accomplish.

Nedra: I've always thought that I had to have a goal to have value as a person. Goals are expectations, and you should have them.

At this point in my life, I lack direction—according to that standard. I've really pulled back a lot. I am getting to the place where I can feel like I've done something valuable with my time, and like I'm a valuable person even though I haven't scratched seven things off a "to do" list.

I used to *do* things all the time, was always gaining ground, accomplishing something, going somewhere. It was my personal expectation for my life that I would *progress.* Now I'm more satisfied to *be.* And yet, there are times when I can become frantic, thinking that I've got to find something to do: a job, a project, a competency.

Sometimes I think I'm raising all those parts of myself that my parents neglected because they were so caught up and focused on expectations. Our family was very event-oriented; the next event was so important. Minutes could never be wasted, everything was timed to the second. What's next? What's on the calendar for today?

So now, I am going back to letting myself waste some time. I can just sit around the house. Or I can go outside and play with my son in the sandbox for an hour and a half and not know it was that long until I came inside. I can get through the day without a list. And my calendar can be more like a diary of what I've done than a planner for what I need to do.

Emily: In order to meet my highest goals, I must have no other goals. My highest goals are to have a happy, cohesive family unit. And in order to do that I have to give up every other goal—such as trying to be showered and dressed by 9:00 every morning, or owning our own home, or making love with a certain amount of regularity. All these things, if I dwell on them, keep me from having what I really want out of life, which is kids that love me and feel secure in our family, a husband who likes coming home to me at night, and fulfilling relationships.

It's . . . Supermom!!!

A friend of Jodi's, the one who suggested I interview her, described Jodi as a "superwoman." I think it was a compliment, although the meaning of that word has become ambiguous in recent years. Superwoman. Supermom. Like "macho"—in the post-Alan Alda, Phil Donahue era, what man wants to be described as "macho"?

Jodi: Maybe my expectations are too high sometimes. *I* don't have a problem with that; other people do.

Why is that?

I think it makes them uncomfortable. They may have doubts about their own situation—are they doing the right thing by staying home with their kids, or are they doing the right thing by working outside the home. I know it's right for me to be home, and I know it's important, and that if it's right and important, it's worth doing to the best of my ability. Other people call that being a superwoman.

In a corporate situation, no one would put you down for trying to be the best and achieve the most. But when I apply this same ambition to my family, then I am put down, and I'm called Superwoman or Supermom, in a negative sense. It can be frustrating. In a corporate situation, I could just come out and say to someone who was criticizing my ambition, "You're saying that because I'm making you look bad by doing so well." But if other women accuse me of doing too well, I can't reply that they're saying it out of jealousy.

I don't like the term *superwoman*. I like to think of myself as someone who's trying to do her best, and I don't like to see a negative label attached to it. I feel that being at home with four children is the most important thing that I'll ever do in my life, and I want to do it well. But anything I do I want to do well—in college I was a Phi Beta Kappa. It's always important for me to do my best.

Lenore: I suppose that people look at our family and wonder how we do it. I still bake all our bread, I still cook everything from scratch; we still eat whole grains and natural foods. I can our garden vegetables. I have my babies at home, I'm home schooling. My children are well-disciplined. I think they wonder how I do it.

How *do* you do it?

I don't know; I guess I just *want* to. If you really want to do something, you will. I want a large family, I want to have our family life be this way.

My expectations for motherhood are actually being exceeded by my reality. Life is better, richer than I had even hoped it would be.

The only thing that's frustrating me right now is a trivial thing: clutter. I haven't been depressed, I don't have the crises about personal fulfillment, I don't go crazy being with the children all day. But I grew up in a clean, tidy house and the fact that I can't keep my house that way is, without a doubt, my biggest frustration and disappointment. It really wears me down.

I get totally horrified when people come over and the house is a mess. I think it reflects on me; they will think I'm a messy person, and I'm really not a messy person, but how can they know that—it sure *looks* like I'm a messy person.

Melissa: Here's an expectation that never gets to the reality stage: I want to bake whole wheat bread with no sugar! When I got married, I thought that no sugar would pass the lips of my children. The reality is that we eat white bread because we all like it better. We put sugar on our cereal and eat store-bought cookies.

We watch too much television, too many videos. We don't have family reading time. My "earth mother" ideal is not being realized.

I had long believed that being a supermom was a positive thing, something I'd work for—to be the best mother I could be. After all, I'd been a super student, a super friend, a super manager at work, a super account executive . . . Why would I want to quit being super when I became a mother? It seemed something noble to strive for.

When the term began to be bantered about in the negative sense, I was (coincidentally?) at the point where I was getting tired of being super, really tired. I was more than happy, then, to join the nay-sayers who mocked women who baked bread, took their children to the zoo every day, bought them flash cards for their birthdays, and read them long story books before bed.

Sue Ellen: People look at me, and maybe they think I'm a superwoman. They think, your kids are fine, your house is gorgeous, you're so organized. Well, my kids are doing okay, my house is nice compared to what most people in the world have. But if I'm having friends over for dinner, you know that I've cleaned my house and laid out an especially nice meal. But that's not the way it is every day!

People come over and say, "You're so relaxed." In a way, that's no compliment. I'm getting so relaxed that I'll let them come over even when things aren't perfect. I didn't used to be that way. I used to kill myself cleaning for hours before I'd invite anyone in.

Anita: I would like to be more emotionally available to my children. I seem to have only so much of myself to go around, between everything that I have to do. I'm not always emotionally available to my kids; I'm more available to my husband because I think that's the most important thing. There are times when they need me, and I wish that I could just tune everything else out and be there for them, but I'm not. I'm tired. So I'm frustrated because I wish I could give more to them.

However, when I was "available" for them because I was home with them all day, I nearly went crazy. Without the chance to be myself and utilize the other gifts God had given me, I would have driven them and myself nuts. I wouldn't have survived it. I was deeply depressed for years, trying to live out something that didn't fit with who I really was. I couldn't be the full-time mother who does everything for her kids. I cried a lot, I was down a lot, I had very little energy, I had all the classic signs of depression.

Candace: My husband sees the physical side of homemaking. When I was working, he would be happy to do his half of the housework, the obvious physical things like dusting or doing dishes or cleaning bathrooms. But of the two of us, I'm the only one who is sensitive to the fact that the kids need to cuddle.

There have been times when I've had to be away for a few days, and when I get back, the house may be immaculate but I have to wonder, what happened with the children? Did they get what they needed in terms of affection and caring? And that's something that you can't put on a list and say, "Here's your half of the nurturing of our children, and here's my half"—the way you can with household chores.

I know that if and when I go back to work, Les will be happy to help with the household chores, but it'll continue to be my job to look after the kids.

My grandmother used to recite this poem—I don't know exactly where it came from, or if I've got it quite right, but it goes like this:

> The woman who lives next door to me
> Is the queerest thing, I think.
> I've seen her sit and read
> With dishes in the sink.
> And many a summer morning,
> She sits rocking in the shade—
> Or makes mud pies with her four-year-old
> And leaves her bed unmade.
> One afternoon, I called on her
> At almost half past four.
> There was dust upon the table
> And muddy tracks on the floor.
> She didn't seem to mind a bit;
> Just laughed and said
> She guessed the work would still be there
> When she was laid to rest.
> I've been doing more important things,
> She smiled.
> She didn't know I'd seen her
> Playing with her child.
> There's no dust upon my table.
> Or muddy tracks upon my floor.
> But, I wonder why the children all love
> That woman who lives next door.

MATERIAL GIRLS, LIVING IN A MATERIAL WORLD

Lucy: I feel societal pressure: being a corporate wife, living in the suburb that's fashionable. For example, it is expected that my daughter will wear Espirit clothes. She's in first grade! There are two little girls, first- and second-graders who ride the bus with Crystal. And in the morning, while they're waiting for the bus, they open their coats and display their clothes and say, "What are you wearing today?" And it's got to be Espirit, right down to the socks.

I took Crystal to Penney's to get some jeans, and she saw a triangle on their Palmetto jeans—which seemed much too expensive for a little girls' jeans to me, anyway—and she said, "Are those Guess? jeans?" I played dumb: "What are Guess? jeans?" Her reply: "Those are the jeans that Kristin wears."

I said, "Well, these are Palmetto jeans, and would you look at that price! Do you know how long you'd have to do your chores to pay for a pair of those jeans?"

There's this tremendous pressure at school. I've heard that the girls will approach each other on the playground, inspect labels, and critique each other on the basis of what the label says. Hmmm . . . I think that this is the first time I've talked about it that my stomach didn't turn. It makes me sick.

We moved to this area because we heard the schools were so good. What a shock this has been! If I had known what it was going to be like, I surely wouldn't have moved into this school district.

There are also these snobbish expectations that go along with Dan's job. At his "level" in the company, there are about four hundred people; there are only thirty places in the next rung up the corporate ladder. So a lot of people are going to be left behind; they won't make it any farther with the company. Consequently, there's a lot of political stuff that goes on, and a lot of positioning within the company. These people do it this way: the wife should be in Junior League; you should belong to a country club or perhaps the sailing club; your kids should be on

the swimming team; the wife should volunteer
for the hospital fashion show. There are lists that
it's good to get your names on.

If you get on these lists, you've arrived. If
you're not on the lists, you haven't arrived—yet.
Or you have no interest. I have no interest. I
suppose people think we're real religious. I know
we're viewed as very religious in our neighborhood, because we're gone Sunday for church.
And we have a Bible study here.

Jolene: My husband is a corporate vice-presi-
dent, and by virtue of his job, we're involved in
"high society." I hate to use those words, but
that's what it is. We go to a lot of fancy dinners
and parties, and I'm expected to entertain at the
drop of a hat—which isn't easy when you have
three kids. I get these calls in the afternoon:
"Honey, how about dinner?" And I'm expected
to lay it on. I have to get the children fed beforehand and know what kinds of foods to serve—
lots of people can't eat seafood, for example—
and I've got to look nice all the time. Which isn't
easy for me, because I have a weight problem. I
have to keep my weight down.

But business relationships are built on friendships. That really is true. I'm very independent,
so it's hard for me. During the year, I go on a few
trips with my husband. I have to look immaculate; the clothing bills for this kind of life! And it's
forced on my children, too. If they're ever along
when we're meeting clients, they have to be perfectly dressed and sit at the table with perfect
manners.

I don't think we've ever taken a vacation
where we didn't have to meet with a client or two
over dinner at some point. You have to take them
to the most expensive restaurant in town, wine

them and dine them, be gracious and understanding, make them feel at ease.

I have two wardrobes: the "me" wardrobe and the wardrobe for Russ's clients. And the children are the same way. They have clothes that I like to see them in and that they like to wear and clothes for when they're seen by Russ's clients.

Candace: I had envisioned us being at the same place my own parents were at this stage in their lives. We aren't. And I don't know if it's just us or if it's the economy of the eighties. My parents started out dirt poor when they were married, and we were, too. But by the time we kids were in grade school, they were getting comfortable. They were in their second house.

We seem to be regressing financially. The house payment gets harder and harder to pay. I expected that because the house payment was more or less the same from year to year, our earnings would go up and it would be easier to pay as time went on. But that's not the case at all. Les went for years without any raise, or just a two percent "cost of living" raise which isn't realistic at all.

Norma: The first years of my marriage to Bill were very, very hard. We didn't have a cent, but we had a whale of a good time. I came into it with very few expectations.

We lived in a small, small apartment. Our kitchen was smaller than my cashier's cage where I worked. We had just enough money to pay the rent, run the car, and eat. We had Sunday dinners at my parents' house; my mother did our laundry. Bill was still in school, but he found that he could study better after we got married because he had better food to eat. When he was single, he lived at a boarding house. He got bed and breakfast—he'd try to eat as much as he could at breakfast—and he kept raisin bread, peanut butter and milk in his car. He ate that for the other two meals of the day.

He was so appreciative of my cooking! Every meal got raves from him. It was a wonderful time in our lives. We were as happy as could be, to have our own little apartment that we could be together in.

I'm sure we didn't analyze things then the way people do now. There are so many books written and so much said about marriage and early marriage and what it ought to be. We didn't think about the adjustments. There *were* adjustments, but we just made them. We worked through them as they came along. We didn't make a major case out of everything that happened in our lives.

Angela: When the "hippie life" came in, I bought it hook, line and sinker—and still do, especially as it concerns money. My father was wealthy, and he used money to show love. I knew, instinctively, that this couldn't be. So I began to view money as something dirty and superficial.

I believe that if you have money, you have heavy responsibilities to it and what it provides. I prefer not to have it.

I'm *trying*, now, to view money as energy and deserving of some respect; as a commodity, produced by creative output, an abundance that comes our way. I would like to believe that it's okay to have it, okay to exchange it for things you like, things you value or that please you aesthetically. I would like to allow money into my life without heavy guilt.

> Still, money seems illicit to me. When I have it, I feel like I'm getting away with a crime. So, I drive an old car—I call it my "humble machine." I *need* an old car; I would really have to go through a lot to have a new car. I'm not sure I could handle it.
>
> It's important for me not to buy into the wealthy suburban life-style, even though I live in a wealthy suburb. I believe I can show character if I reject the materialism.

Jolene recognizes a private identity separate from the personna she must project for her husband's clients and business associates; it's expressed in her "me" and "them" wardrobes. I admire her for making this distinction. I'm a little more like Angela in the sense that I believe my character (and my value) is caught up in my possessions. I say, to my shame, that I feel worthwhile when I have "stuff," and worthless when I don't.

The stuff may be money, possessions, status, education, expertise . . . they all get caught up in who I am.

Denise told me, "I'm trying to get free of the belief that I am what I accomplish or that I am what other people think of me. I don't want those things to be the measure of my worth." I wish that—exactly. But it's hard for me, because for my whole life I have been able to accomplish things. So how can I find a sense of worth outside these tangibles?

What I Do, Who I Am

> **Kerri:** All my life, I've identified myself by what I do. First it was who I was married to, then the job that I did—right down to having a business card to prove what I did—and all these other

relationships and jobs that I *did*. The lesson, for me, is this: I am a child of God, and that's enough. That's more than enough—that's great.

Irene: When I was sick in the hospital, I couldn't do anything. I could hardly say thank you when something was done for me. And that experience helped to show me that I don't have to *do* anything to deserve God's love and approval. He just gives it to me; it's grace.

I can't say my experience has cut down a lot on the doing—I still do a lot. But the *value* of what I do is different.

Suzanne: I went into therapy twenty years ago because I was concerned about the Vietnam War; specifically, I was angry because I couldn't stop it. This was just one issue, though, and it spoke of a greater issue, which was that I felt I had no control over my life or the events that were shaping my life.

I have always believed that as human beings, there ought to be some way that we can control our destiny. Now, I am doing things that make a difference. [Suzanne is a state senator.] I am making life better in my state and making things better for my friends. So I can say that even though I certainly have a lot of unfinished business, if I were to die today, I could die happy because I've finally found a way to make a difference in the world. Granted, there are a million problems that I'm not solving, but I can live with that when there are a dozen problems that I *am* solving.

Helen: I am able to define myself in terms that have nothing to do with the relationship I'm in, or what other people perceive me to be. So many women can only define themselves relationally: I'm a mother, or a wife, or a volunteer, or a boss, or a friend. It doesn't mean I'm not relational, because I am. But I don't live to please people. My survival has rested on listening to my own gut and doing what I thought was best.

The "people pleasers" struggle with guilt, because that has to do with what they *do* and how other people judge those actions. I struggle with shame, because shame has to do with who I *am*.

As long as I *can* "do" it's hard for me to know what it means just to "be." Irene had all the "doing" knocked out of her when she was in the hospital with serious heart disease, and the experience helped her see how much God loves Irene, not what Irene does. A sudden event gave her (relatively) sudden understanding.

Kerri, on the other hand, has been working on that truth as a ten-year-long lesson, gradually growing into understanding.

In the end, we all need to comprehend the message of grace, however it comes to us.

Robin: People look to the Bible for what they can *do*, but I think that Scripture tells us what we are to *be*, not what we are to *do*. And that's where people get frustrated with it. Because they want to be told what to do; it's easier. But to *be* like Christ . . . if that's what you strive to *be*, then you're on the right track.

HELEN'S STORY

Helen is a fifty-one-year-old beauty who lives in a cedar-and-glass house overlooking the rugged canyons of southern California. A charmed life? It certainly looked perfect to me; she looked perfect to me. Yet Helen's story is filled with disappointment and pain, dreams that have died. Twice married, mother of three children, she is weighing the risk of marriage to her boyfriend, Patrick.

My mother married my father, had me, and divorced him less than a year after I was born. I didn't know him. When I was about two, she married my stepfather, and they had my two brothers.

This was in the thirties, and there was a lot of shame attached to being divorced; the fact that she had a baby made it obvious that she was divorced. My mother was ashamed of me. She was always saying, "Your father doesn't support you, he never sends any money for you. Your stepfather supports you; he doesn't have to do this—you ought to be real grateful." At four years old, how could I be grateful to my stepfather for the food on my plate?

My brothers were the *real* children, and I was a second-class citizen. Some of it might have had to do with me being a girl, but mostly it was my mother's shame. What she had not resolved within herself came to me. I knew that I reminded her of my father, and she didn't like him.

When I was about eight or nine years old, I remember thinking, *If I believe I'm who she says I am, I'm going to die. Therefore, I am not going to believe her*. From that time on, I was my own person.

That's not to say she couldn't hurt me. She could. If I had a date or somewhere to go, she'd come into my room beforehand and pick a fight with me, and I'd have to leave the house upset, red-eyed. That happened quite a bit. I know that I was everything she wasn't: She was shy, withdrawn, not very pretty. She'd say to me, "I don't know why the boys like you, Helen. Heaven knows you're not a pretty girl." I could be hurt by it, to be sure. But never again did I really internalize her opinion of me. I simply couldn't. I couldn't afford to believe that I really was a piece of dirt.

To this day, I really am affected very little by what other people think of me.

PURSUING THE DREAM

I wanted to be the mother I never had. I wanted children, badly. So, at the age of twenty-two, when my plans for traveling and being a beatnik weren't panning out, all I could think of was that if I got married, I could have children, and then I'd be happy. I wanted children more than I wanted a husband. I had problems with my ovaries and knew there was a chance I couldn't conceive. But this just made me more determined to try anyway while time was still on my side.

I remember lying in bed, praying: "God, please send me a husband so I can have children. If you do, I'll be good. I'll wash the floors and change the sheets every week; I'll learn to be a good cook, I'll do all those things." I was willing to do all these domestic tasks, all these things which were so "un-intellectual," and I was making a bargain with God that I'd completely shut off my intellectual, freedom-loving side if he'd just give me children.

I got what I prayed for. I married a young man I'd met in college. As it turned out, I was *not* able to conceive, so as soon as we could, we adopted a child, and then we adopted another. Three years after the second adoption, I had a miracle birth; with only a little piece of one ovary left, I was able to conceive. It was such an impossibility, I didn't even go to the doctor until I was five months' pregnant. I thought I had cancer, and I was going to be real brave; I never considered that I might be pregnant.

I was *not* the mother I thought I would be. I carried into motherhood all the inadequacies and limitations I had grown up with. My marriage was going pretty well; my husband and I had similar backgrounds, similar intellectual capabilities, and were compatible, but he became alcoholic. When I realized that he was alcoholic, the marriage went downhill fast.

My *expectations* were that I would get married, be a good girl, be a good mother, and my husband would take care of me, and it would be forever. But one day, after thirteen years of marriage, he came home from work and asked for a divorce. We tried marriage counseling, but that wasn't getting us very far. And then he became very sick and was hospitalized, and in the course of going through his things, I found out that he had a girlfriend.

It never occurred to me to forgive and forget, to attribute it to the alcoholism. It never occurred to me to do anything but get out. I thought I was the victim. The marriage wasn't my responsibility anymore.

The alcoholism had made things very difficult. I can't say he ever beat me, but he was very abusive. There was a lot of yelling, a lot of threatening . . . and it came from nowhere. Once when we were having a terrible argument, and the kids were roaming around the house—they were seven, five and two—he threw me down on the living room floor and raped me. I felt that I had to give in to him—I couldn't fight too much, because I didn't want the children to come in and see what was happening.

It was something I repressed for many years because of my shame. I actually felt *responsible* for it, like it was my fault. I believed what most women believe: that the relationship, the family, is their responsibility, and if something goes bad, they're to blame.

I was so bitter, so confused. I felt that I had done my part; I couldn't figure out why it wasn't working out. What was going wrong?

I *did* get a divorce. It was a hard time. I remember that Helen Reddy's song, "I Am Woman," was real popular then. I had the record, and I played it until the hole in the middle was about an inch across. I just rallied to that song.

When I became single again, I still identified with my mother role. Mothers don't go out and party. They sure don't sleep around. It never could fit with who I was and what I was.

I was lucky, because my ex-husband made good money, and he was faithful in sending it to me. What he didn't do was attend to his children. In the nine years following our divorce, he saw them nine times. He abandoned them.

I was finding it difficult to be mother and father to my three children. It was really hard. Being single was hard, so I married for the second time.

I wanted so badly to have a father for my children that I denied the reality of the man who was my husband. I projected onto him all the things that I needed him to be. I really believed that we had a great relationship, that I was very much in love with him, but I was convincing myself of these things because I needed them to be true. I needed him to be something he wasn't.

He was not a father to my children—he had no interest in them. He would not support me financially, and I realized that when the child support money ran out, I'd be in big trouble. I *knew* that I had to take care of myself, and I essentially vowed that I'd never be financially dependent on a man again. I moved our family to California (husband and children), bought a business, and started aggressively investing everything I could in real estate. And I've gotten enough so that I've got freedom —not a fur coat, not a new luxury car, but enough security so that I don't have to stay with a man just because he can pay my bills.

"KEEP YOUR COTTON-PICKIN' HANDS OFF"

Those years were very difficult. I had to send my oldest son away to high school because he couldn't get along with my husband. My next son, who had had a history of problems like learning disabilities, became heavily involved with drugs. My daughter had emotional and psychological problems, mostly related to her father's abandonment.

Some children just sail through adolescence, but I believe there will always be a payday. At some point, those kids are going to have to question the values that their parents taught them, and they're probably going to rebel.

I believe something now that I wish I had known before: you have to keep your hands off your kids' lives when they're going through a rough adolescence. You have to practice benign neglect. Grit your teeth, and keep your cotton-pickin' hands off. I really wish I had done that more. It would have been painful, but they would have learned sooner and better.

Tell me how you coped with your son's drug dependency.

I think I did all the normal things. I did the Alcoholics Anonymous thing. I laid down rules, I searched his room, I told him that I could not control his drug use outside the home, but if he used drugs in my house he could no longer live here. When that happened, I threw him out. I had a tremendous fear that he wouldn't live through it.

Someone told me that you have to be willing to see your child dead on the side of the road. That's how tough it has to get, because otherwise it's certain death. Somehow, you have to keep your hands off the natural consequences of their drug abuse.

We got him into a drug treatment program, and he acted so badly they kicked him out. I wouldn't let him come back home, so he started living with friends of his who were on drugs. He ended up with his dad, who was single at the time and still drinking.

Eventually, his father put him into a long-term drug treatment program in Hawaii. They shaved the kids' heads, shouted and screamed obscenities at them; it was real rough. They were saying, "You're tough? We'll show you what tough is."

He's learned a lot. I feel thankful that he's reached the age of twenty-one. He's been drug-free for two and a half years.

I spent years protecting my children, but all of a sudden I couldn't do that anymore. Not in any way. I felt like such a failure, as though if I'd "done it right" I could have prevented it all. If I'd only done it right, if I'd only married the right man . . .

I'm not real close to my son right now. He lives with his father in another city. Our values are very different. He's very materialistic, he's bright. Part of my dream is that we'll be close again.

I've been on a serious spiritual journey. I wanted to find out what in the world had happened with my life. Why was it in a shambles?

It occurred to me that instead of blaming my mother, or my first husband, or my second husband, or my children . . . maybe I should take a look inside myself and see what was there. After living with an alcoholic man, I, too, had become alcoholic. As I got treatment for my alcoholism, I was challenged to give the whole thing over to the Lord, which I did. I just gave him my problem, and thank God, it was taken away from me. I didn't have the withdrawl that many people do.

The twelve-step program AA teaches is an inner journey. There's the reliance on a higher power. You must go back over your life from Day One and think of whom you may have harmed and make amends when you can. There's confession, to God and to another human being, which is a wonderful release. The program teaches that even though other people may have had a part in our problems, we can only make progress if we look at ourselves and what *we* can do to change.

I had such bitterness toward my mother, and I knew it was killing me. I had to do something about it, though I could not forgive her. I *pretended* to forgive her, but it would always come up again—that gall, that horrible feeling.

But then a friend said, "Just pray for her. You don't have to forgive her, God will forgive her for you." So every time I would think of my mother, I'd pray, "God, give my mother every happiness and joy." It was very insincere at first; I just said the words and didn't really mean it. Along the line, something very wonderful happened: she was forgiven, and I did not do it. The bitterness and pain I'd carried for thirty years went away.

I've been in counseling, taken personality profile tests, read books, studied different theories. These are all just tools, possible ways of reaching wholeness. In the end, I want to be like Jesus. He's my model.

I'm striving for a God-consciousness. I want to be God-centered every minute of the day, and that's what I strive toward. It's impossible, of course, but that's where I'm heading anyway.

I know that I can only approach this goal, so when I fall short of it, I don't berate myself too much.

THE DREAM

The thing that is so maddening about my first husband isn't that he betrayed me by having a mistress, it isn't that he was an alcoholic, but it's that he killed my dream. I've never been able to forgive him for it.

I'm still struggling with that dream. The dream is that you fall in love, have babies, do all the homey things, the holiday family things, you go to church, pray together, your children get older, there's a picture of their graduation, you do things together, you grow closer, you love each other unconditionally, and you grow old together. You enjoy your grandchildren together. Totally unrealistic, I guess, but that's what I wanted and that's what I don't have, and I can't forgive Winston for killing that dream.

I don't know how it is for men, but I would think that the burden of providing this for a woman would be almost intolerable. To live with a woman who is living out that dream . . . it must be terribly difficult for a man who doesn't have the dream.

Now, what I want now is someone to grow old with. Sometimes I run from the commitment of this relationship I'm in, but I want someone to grow old with, so it's worth whatever price I pay. Part of the price I pay is that I become more honest. I look at what I want, and what I've got, and I say, "Well, that's the dream part. That's the part that isn't likely to happen for me." Unconditional love—that's a dream. I've wanted it in the past, but I see now that when I love, I love conditionally. And I am loved conditionally. That's reality. Even as a mother I don't love unconditionally. The best I can do is be that clear and open channel that God can love through. That's as good as it gets. I *can* love unconditionally through him.

I still have a dream, yes. Life *is* better when it's shared. There's a lot of wisdom in the old adage that when you share trouble, it's halved, and when you share joy, it's doubled.

I've survived enough in my life that I don't have fears about the future anymore. I know that whatever comes my way, I'll be able to say, "This, too, shall pass" because it will. I've seen problems come and go, and I know that they don't stay around forever. So whatever the future holds for me, I know I'm equal to the task.

As far as my expectations for life were concerned, it didn't pan out at all. Nobody ever told me that I'd have to watch out for myself the way I did. Nobody ever told me it might be a good idea to have a little money of my own, because men sometimes leave their women.

My life has been painful, but I don't have any regrets. I'm happy with who I am, and in the midst of the pain there has been joy, too. Lots of learning, lots of growth.

Human beings carry their own baggage. My picture of my life is carrying a heavy pack and just unloading rocks as I go along. I'm tossing them over my shoulder, and the burden is really quite light right now. Those rocks are inflated expectations and unrealistic dreams.

I believe that there is a tremendous amount of joy in this world. My *tendency* is to try to figure everything out, and if things are wrong I tend to find a way to fix them, to make them right. But if I can just relax and take things as they come and appreciate them for what they are, it makes all the difference in the world as to how people treat me and what kind of relationship I have with them. Very often, it's important for me to keep my hands out of the pot and just let it simmer on its own. If I can be here now and live this day today, then I can have real joy.

CHAPTER TEN

Disappointment and Serendipity

There's a wonderful line in the movie *Broadcast News*. The fast-track newscaster asks his rival, "What do you do when your life surpasses your wildest dreams?"

"Keep it to yourself."

*I*s it easier to share our disappointments than to exclaim over the happy surprises that life brings? I find that when I am enjoying an unexpected pleasure, an unsought success or a windfall of happiness, there is a chorus of unspoken advice: "Keep it to yourself."

"What has been your biggest disappointment" and "What has been your most pleasant surprise?"—these two questions usually came at the end of my interviews, as the answers come at the end of this book. To identify disappointments and serendipity—that unlooked-for blessing—points to unrealized expectations: either expectations of success, or expectations of nothing special.

Most women could identify disappointments. Some were general: "I guess I just thought that life wouldn't be this complicated," and "I expected life to be rewarding and fulfilling. I had no idea that it would be so *hard*, that there would be so much unhappiness and suffering."

Other disappointments were specific: "I suppose my biggest disappointment was losing our baby. We had certainly expected that everything would go perfectly." Indeed, the death of a close friend or relative was a long-term, lingering disappointment for many: "The biggest disappointment of my life was my mother's death. I was devastated for two years afterward. I don't mean disappointed for two months; I mean absolutely devastated for a full two years after she died. My failed marriage, that's certainly a disappointment. Not finishing college—on bad days it seems like a big disappointment. But my mother's death is a continuing disappointment."

A death is absolutely final, completely irreversible; I'm not surprised that it emerges as a major disappointment, because the grieving person is powerless to change the reality. But perhaps the "might have been" dreams are just as painful, because they carry with them all sorts of second thoughts, backward looks and "if only" regrets:

> **Lois:** I had some dreams that haven't come true. I had always hoped that Peter and I would be able to go to Europe together, that we could retire together—have a home in the South where we could spent winters—and that we'd enjoy growing old together. But he died, and that dream died.
>
> I had always thought that if I had the time, I could write. But I see now that if I really had it in me to write, I would find time to do it. If you're a writer, you write. Just like if you're a reader, you read.

I had a pretty good voice when I was young and got a lot of encouragement from voice teachers. I thought that maybe I would do more singing. But when the children were little, I was so tired that I couldn't sing; my voice simply wouldn't be there because I was exhausted. And over the years I realized that I was losing my voice and that I wouldn't have that in my life. I thought I might do more gospel singing, but that never panned out.

WHITE KNIGHTS WHO FELL OFF THEIR HORSES

Monica: I think the crushing thing for me was the fact that my husband didn't want me to quit my job—even when the strain of working and raising a family had gotten me to the point where I was hospitalized in a mental hospital. He depended on my paycheck, and if I quit working, it was a threat to him. He didn't want me to stay home and raise my children.

Florence: It's very, very hard for me to accept the areas that Mark is weak in—it's a real loss, in a way, of what I had hoped. When I got married, I thought, *This man is going to take care of me.* As it's turned out, he wanted me to take care of him.

When things went wrong, I thought he'd come up to me and say, "Honey, let's sit down and figure this out," like they do on the soap operas. He would listen and come up with good solutions and then give me a hug. But it's not that way for me, and I don't know any marriages that are like that. Men don't do that, I guess, but that's not what I supposed when I got married.

Karen: After we had been married for two years, Bob lost his job. He was in a highly specialized field, and he couldn't find anything that fit with his training. He got depressed, seriously depressed. I would be working all day, and he'd be home. I'd get back to the house and he'd be lying on the couch, with dishes stacked high in the sink, junk all over the floor. And he'd ask, "What's for dinner?" That was a very hard time . . . I couldn't understand why he couldn't at least keep up the house since he wasn't working.

My dad would call, and say, "Isn't Bob working . . . yet?" I had pretty much lost my desire to be married to this man, who was so different on account of his unemployment. And then he got a job, in another city one thousand miles away. He was going to go ahead while I stayed behind to sell the house and wrap up our affairs. I let him go without the least feeling of loss. I thought, *Fine.*

But, once he was gone, I had a terrific sense of loss. I knew that I really wanted to be with him. I had accumulated so many negative feelings about him when he was an unemployed slob, but when we were apart I realized that I wanted and needed to be with him. I started thinking about the things I loved about him. After four weeks, we quit being blasé about our separation. And two weeks after that I was with him in our new home. When we were reunited, it was like a honeymoon, like starting over again. We were in love. It was wonderful. We were living in an efficiency apartment with a fold-out sofa, a card table to eat on, and that was our furniture. It was so romantic. We had each other.

Later, Bob told me that his parents had gone through a couple of separations. When I met his parents, they were lovebirds: they held hands, and he opened her car door, and they kissed in public—something I had never seen my parents or any of their friends do. But they had been through some tough times that they chose to work through, and it had made their marriage stronger.

Lenore: My dad went to work at 8:00, was home at 4:30. He never worked at night, never on the weekends. I didn't ever verbalize it, but I certainly had it in my head that Monte would be home in the evenings and on the weekends. He's a minister, and weekends are pretty much devoted to church work. And in the evenings he does need to go visiting; lots of his parishioners are tied up during the day, and evenings are when they're free.

We've worked this out pretty much, but it hasn't been easy. I keep thinking, *Hey, what about me?*

When Monte was between churches and was working for minimum wage for over four years, it was hard. He was asking himself, "Who am I? I'm not a pastor." There was certainly a money crunch, but as I look back on it, it's really wonderful the way the Lord took care of us. Monte worked thirty-two hours a week, minimum wage, and we had two children—but we never missed out on anything important. We had enough.

But as the whole thing dragged on, I did despair a bit. I decided I didn't want to have any more children, because I just didn't feel I had anything to offer more kids.

I didn't know that Monte would have to work at different jobs, that we'd be moving around, that his hours were be so unusual. I guess all of it has been good for growth; we've really had to trust the Lord, and trust each other.

ABANDONED WOMEN

In Chapter **8**, **Cheryl** described the rejection of her church when she decided to divorce her husband. Here, she backs up and tells us more about that marriage—what she thought she was getting into, what actually happened. It's a story of emotional abandonment and abuse.

> When I got married, I thought I had a guaranteed, happily-ever-after deal. My husband was the first Christian I had ever known. I met him at a time when I really wanted to know God. He represented strength to me. I thought he would take care of me. He was very religious; he looked godly. He talked about God constantly; he preached in the streets, was very charismatic, and would draw a huge crowd.

> I had only known him two months before we got married. I needed someone, and he promised to be that person.

> We had been married for about a week when he hit me the first time. He had a violent temper. I don't even know what it was about—something small; I just crossed him.

> I expected that I would meet a man, fall in love, have children, and live happily ever after. We did have five children. And I can remember, once, sitting in the car in the driveway thinking how wonderful it was to have a family. Because growing up, it had been just me and my dad. I missed having a mom, and having brothers and sisters.

> Conflict wouldn't have bothered me, if we'd been able to talk. I don't have to have people agreeing with me, but I have to be heard. I have to know they're listening. He would not listen.

And he would not enter into conflict. He was very immature.

Whenever we had a problem, whenever I would introduce a conflict, he'd either start singing—very loud singing—or he'd turn on the radio real loud or he'd leave. And if he felt he was losing his temper, which meant losing control, he could become very violent. He could put me down emotionally by quoting Scripture at me, or using God to intimidate me.

He'd quote Corinthians, saying that the Bible said, "Let those who have wives be as if they had none," and use it as an excuse for not meeting my needs. He told me what books to read, what music to listen to, what clothes to wear. He was very rigid in terms of his church attendance and his daily disciplines: he'd read a chapter of the Bible every day, pray exactly an hour every day. And he expected me to do this, too.

For a while, it was okay. Eight years later I woke up and said, "What about me? Am I a person? Do I matter?" All hell broke loose. I had a need to *be* someone. When I realized what was happening, things got much worse. I no longer wanted to be dictated to; I no longer wanted to be told what to do, what to wear, how to act.

I held God responsible for all the pain in my marriage; I associated him very closely with everything that was happening to me. The God I fell in love with when I got married was the God I ended up hating.

In my innocence, I thought that my marriage was what a Christian marriage was supposed to be. Brad didn't believe in fellowship; he thought it was a waste of time for Christians to get together. Consequently, I was very isolated. It was a Christian marriage to me: the husband told the wife what to do, and that was called submission.

I had a dull ache all through my marriage. After my divorce, it became a sharp pain. Divorce went against everything I believed in. I was raised Catholic, and I could hardly accept it. I believed marriage was for the rest of my life, and I couldn't see any way out.

I clearly remember one incident. Brad took me to a carnival where he was going to be preaching. We got separated, because he was preaching and I was doing something else, and it got to be about 11:00 at night and I was frantically looking for him. But he had gone home! He had just left me there, with no way to get back. Finally, I found a guy that could take me home. It was 11:30 when I got home, and he got mad at me for waking him up! At that point I realized, *This person doesn't care for me one bit.*

That happened after four years of marriage. Still, I expected that things would get better. I figured I was doing something wrong, and as soon as I could do it all better, then the marriage would get better. If I would submit more, read the Bible more, pray more, get it together somehow.

In the meantime everything just got worse. He continued to be abusive. I'm sure I would have gotten hit a lot more if I hadn't learned how to back off when he was losing control of his temper.

We lived in a bad neighborhood, a dangerous neighborhood, and often when Brad traveled I would be afraid of being alone with the children in the house. But one night, as I was lying in bed, I realized that I was more afraid of my husband lying next to me than I was of whoever might be outside the window, whoever might want to rape or kill me. Because he was so unpredictable, I never knew what was going to set him off, when he'd get angry, or what he'd do when he was angry.

It got so that I'd cry for an hour or two every night after the kids were in bed. Sometimes he'd come up to my room and hassle me, sometimes he'd leave me alone. But I'd cry every night. I kept trying to do better, trying to be better; I read the books, listened to the tapes, attended the services . . . trying to find out what it was that I could do that would make this person love me and care for me.

After eight or nine years, I finally began to see that it wasn't my fault, and that I couldn't fix it. This guy had problems. I spent a couple years in this transitional place, trying to piece it all together, trying to figure out what it all meant. My love died, and when that happened, I spent less effort trying to figure out how to be better and more effort trying to survive. The pain got sharper. Then I went numb.

If he had just not met my needs, I think I'd still be married. But it was the constant battering, the emotional battering, the beating down, the criticism, that I couldn't take any longer. I became agoraphobic, I couldn't be in groups, I hated church, hated God, couldn't pray. It's only been in the last six months that I can hear someone quote Scripture or talk about God without cringing involuntarily.

I would like to be able to go into church without fear. I'm working on that, just like an alcoholic might work on going into a bar without fear. But the fear is still with me. I have to work through it every time I attend worship or pick up the Bible.

I had so many questions. How could I be a Christian and be filled with so much conflict? How can I be the very thing I hate? What I've decided is that, yeah, I did want to be a Christian. So I'm going to work through all this stuff. It's not easy. How can I work through hatred of everything I am and want to be? But I'm still doing it. I'm in the process.

Theresa has felt abandoned by her entire family. At a time in her life when she began to have her own needs, she found that her husband and children weren't there for her—and that situation continues. And Lois tells us what it was like to walk through a terminal illness with her husband and then be left behind when death demanded his life.

Theresa: I am so unhappy and discouraged and absolutely confused about my children. I gave and nurtured them to such a degree that I expected it to knit us together as a family. I gave everything to my family and my husband; I put myself last.

I went through a crisis when I was thirty-nine, and I expected that my family would be there for me. Sometimes I didn't feel like I could cook supper or do the food shopping—I was depressed. But they weren't supportive at all, and that was a shock.

When I became needy, nobody could give. My husband couldn't give, my children couldn't give—they don't care. There is a lack of respect for me as I get older, no return of caring. When I express my needs, I get no response. None.

I can usually cope pretty well. I can see things coming ahead of time, plan for them, and deal with them when they arrive. But if this is happening to me . . . it's got to be happening to lots of women. This is a major cultural phenomenon, and I'm sure lots of women are having to deal with it. I'll tell you, being raised in the fifties has not prepared me to be a woman in the eighties.

It's possible that I gave too much; I'm changing now. For example, not one person in my family has ever come to a service at the church I pastor. Not in three years, and the services are just across the street here! Now, is that ludicrous? Why can't they come? My sons haven't come, my daughter hasn't come, my husband hasn't come. How can they do that? How can people do that? What are they afraid of? What are the real issues?

I may have given too much, sure. But I think that if you don't stay in the traditional role, you risk this kind of rejection.

They say, "Oh, you don't cook for us anymore." The main thing I hear from my husband is, "You don't cook," because caring means cooking and cleaning and being in the house all the time. So if I have a life of my own, they can't accept it; they see it almost as adultery.

In my family the accepted thing is that the mother puts food on the table—pasta and ravioli and steak—and this is the way she says she loves her family.

But I'm not doing that now, and it's hard for my kids to understand. Food they could understand. But we're developing a new kind of relationship. I show them I love them by talking about things with them, by being involved in their lives. In doing this, I realize that I'm on a hard road, because it means that I have to earn their respect. If I was going to love them with food and a clean house, I could just get it automatically.

I wanted to have children, and I'd do it again. But what I'd do different is this: I wouldn't expect them to give me anything in return.

I am getting what I need emotionally from sources outside my family, as hard as that has been to do. I get support from a counselor I see, from a Bible study group I belong to, from other people. Friends. It's an incredible identity crisis—that I should find family outside my true family. I thought my family would be my life.

I'm not a mother like I expected to be; I'm not a mother-in-law like I expected to be; I don't even look like I expected to look at the age of forty-nine. I don't think like I expected to think. I have more life now than I ever did—more interests, more stimulating circumstances in one day than I used to have in a month.

Lois: A never-to-be-forgotten experience was being with my husband during his last illness. For three and a half months he had cancer. People always expect cancer to last for a year or two, but he was diagnosed, and three and a half months later he was dead. I was with him as much as I could be—that's what he wanted.

Yet, there was a distance. There were times I felt that he was living on another planet, another world, that he'd already left this life.

But when he actually died, I felt that I'd been walking hand-in-hand with him for a long time; that we'd walked up a very steep hill, trudged laboriously up to the top; and that at the top of the hill there was a gate that swung open as we reached it. It opened, and he went through, and then the gate slammed shut in my face. He had gone, and I was left behind. I was surprised—shocked—to be left alone.

I had related so to his illness, I was almost breathing with him. It was a shock to see him go. And then I looked around me and there was so much to do—pick a casket, schedule the funeral, call people, choose pallbearers. Doorbells ringing, people coming.

FACING THE DISAPPOINTMENTS

DeAnn: I can see a positive side to disappointment. We tend to give our lives to those things that will give life back to us. We invest in our children because we think they will love us back; we devote ourselves to our marriages because we think we'll get love in return; we give ourselves to friendships, work, whatever. But invariably and inevitably we are disappointed. People let us down; jobs let us down; relationships let us down. And when they do—and it always happens—God is still there. When our other interests and loves disappoint us, it's a way for us to see that we simply cannot put our trust in these things. It's a reminder of where our highest devotion should be placed—in God.

I used to think that even God wasn't there in the disappointment—that even he didn't love me, that he would disappoint me like the others. But that's pretty much a settled issue with me now. Once in a while I still have the doubt, but God's really done some major changes with me on the inside. When the people I love and depend upon most disappoint me, then it's a time when I look to God and realize, yet again, that he's always there for me. To know that makes such a difference.

What if there isn't a sunny side, a silver lining to the cloud? Must we keep insisting that there is? As I become more realistic about life and what it holds for us, I'm seeing that the disappointments can't always be dressed up to look good. Not every failure eventually brings us to a place of success. Some failures are absolutely miserable, absolutely devastating.

> **Cheryl:** A lot of my Christian friends try to cheer me up. They say, "Hey, everything is going to work out just fine. It all works together for good. You just hang in there and read your Bible and pray, and God will see you through this."
>
> They won't let me experience my disappointment. They can't handle the failure of it themselves, and they don't want me to deal with it either. There is this pressure to keep looking okay, like everything is going to be all right.
>
> But we're not all going to live happily ever after. We aren't going to be okay. Life is hard. It gets rough, and then it gets rougher. It's full of disappointments and disillusionments.
>
> Yet some of my friends can't accept this. They keep up with this naive optimism. And it creates tremendous conflict in me. Because I know, deep down, that I am right about life being difficult.

If there is no silver lining in the tragedies of life, there is at least consolation, as DeAnn shared: "The Lord's helping me to look at life more realistically, to not have such unrealistic expectations. To be honest about my pain. 'Blessed are those who mourn, for they shall be comforted. Blessed are the poor in spirit.' If you don't ever mourn, you're not a candidate for comfort. There needs to be an honesty about the pain and disappointment if we're to heal."

Patricia: A lot of what I don't like, I have to just take on the chin. That's life, and there's nothing you can do about it. We have to make our peace with the way this world is, and with the faults of the people around us. I can fly into a rage when my daughter lies to me; there's a part of me that thinks, *This just can't be. This person cannot have this fault. She shouldn't do this wrong thing.* Or if George says for months that he'll do some project around the house, but never seems to get around to it. I could get eaten up with it.

But it's wrong for me to hold it against them. I do things that they don't like; I expect them to put up with me, and I need to put up with them, even if I might wish that they were different.

Lynelle: I've had a couple hard knocks. My only brother died when he was a teenager. A few years ago, I was physically attacked by my neighbor. It was horrible. During the whole thing, which took place in my own home, I just prayed to God to save me and protect me.

But you have to go on from there. I could have let either one of those things become an excuse for my whole life, and people would have understood. But what good would it do me?

If you're an unhappy, complaining young woman . . . you're going to grow to be an unhappy, complaining old woman. I don't want to be the kind of person who bangs her head against the wall over something like a death and doesn't accept God's love and healing. This doesn't mean that I'll accept anything, be submissive, turn into a door mat. What it means is I can't be happy if I insist on fighting the same old battles my whole life.

In a way, it's rebellion against God. You're saying, "I'm not going to accept healing and forgiveness. I'm going to keep it alive forever and forever, no matter what. I'm going to let it rule my life and make everybody else miserable, too."

When things go wrong, you have to say, "Okay, where am I now, what have I got left, and what can I do?" and then you have to move on. You decide to live. Maybe a marriage is over, maybe a child is gone, maybe a dream has died. You can cry and wring your hands for twenty years *if you want*, but that's a choice. You can also choose to put it behind you and look at your other options and rebuild your life from there.

If you have six choices, it's no good being angry because the seventh one isn't available to you. You just have to look at your six options and do what you can with what you have.

AT LAST, A FEW HAPPY SURPRISES

Jodi: My marriage has turned out better than I thought it would. And I was hoping for the best!

Hazel: I didn't expect my husband to be so wonderful. Of course, when we were dating I knew he was great, but I had no idea how great he really was. I married the national treasure, but I had no idea at the time. We've been married for almost forty years, and around there they call us the sweethearts on campus. So not only is he a treasure, but he still loves me. I keep praying that God will keep Lawrence's blinders on!

I didn't expect my two daughters to be so beautiful, or that they'd be such tremendous friends. They're my best friends. And if you were to ask them who their best friend is, they'd say me.

And I'm surprised that God has used me the way he has. I never expected to have these opportunities for ministry.

Barbara: One very big, wonderful surprise has been the love I've received from friendships. I never expected to be so valued and cared for by my friends. Most of the healing in my life has not come from me; I haven't engendered it. But it's come from friends. I've been blessed, throughout my adult life, with unusual, terrific people, who have put their hooks in me and not let go. God has put so many of these people in my life—more than most people have, I think—that I see it as a special blessing he's given me.

Juliet: One of the big surprises of motherhood has been how much joy it brings. I think I was more prepared for the work and the physical exhaustion than I was for the fun of having Danielle in our lives. We were married for five years before we decided to have a child. If we'd known how nice it was going to be, I think we would have tried sooner.

Lois: It was not my expectation that after nineteen years of widowhood, at the age of seventy-four, that I would remarry. I was finally reconciled to being single, finally at peace with it. And looking back now on the decision to remarry, I can see that there were a lot of things I didn't check into or investigate, such as my compatibility with my new husband. But I felt and feel that it was exactly the right thing to do, that it's in God's will. And if I had decided to say no to this marriage, it would be like saying no to life, and to God's presence in my life, and to growth.

CHAPTER ELEVEN

Speaking the Truth

*S*trangely, only after the interviewing was over did it occur to me to ask myself how *I* might have responded to my own questions. What are my disappointments and happy surprises? These questions and their answers were only a vague tangle of thoughts and feelings before I commenced on this project.

For example, it wasn't until I had heard several women tell how, as teenagers, they were discouraged from pursuing a college education or any life that took them out of the traditional wife-and-mother role, that I pondered the encouragement of my own family while growing up.

There was my grandmother who lived with us when I was young, and who told me, "Alice, remember this: don't be the nurse, be the doctor. Don't be the secretary, be the lawyer." A strong admonition, delivered by a woman who had herself been a legal secretary at the turn of the century when it was definitely "men's work"—and a mildly scandalous pursuit for a young woman in her day.

And her daughter, my mother, who had received the same encouragement as a child, never steered me away from anything difficult or ambitious. The sky was my limit. What a shock it was for her when I attended a non-prestigious college to study nursing (not pre-med), then married at the age of eighteen and worked as a secretary to put my husband through school. Hardly what she had in mind! Hardly her desire for her youngest child and only daughter—the "frosting on the cake."

Who can measure the effect these women had on my expectations for life? Who can measure the influence of three older brothers who doted on me constantly, tutored me through grade school, taught me to throw a football correctly ("No, Alice, you're throwing like a *girl*!"), and at the same time taught me to allow a gentleman to open my doors? Can you imagine spending the first five years of life being called "The Queen of Santa Fe"?

Since it was my own family, the only one I knew, it is only natural I imagined every little girl being told by her parents and siblings that she could do and be absolutely anything she wanted—as long as it was something spectacular!

TAPPING REALITY

This book is the result of a simple idea and a straightforward undertaking: to ask women of faith about their expectations for life and how the expectations are matching up with reality. This is not the last word on the subject, far from it. Only fifty women have been interviewed—so many more voices might have been heard, so many more stories told.

My credentials for this endeavor are modest. I am not a trained journalist or counselor. At most, I am what some call a "born bartender," the kind of person others confide in comfortably.

The scope of the book is fairly modest, too: a few thoughts about expectations and reality, dreams and disappointments. Not life, the universe and everything.

Still, it's a start. For many of the women I talked to, the interview itself was a first step toward some degree of critical thinking about the influences and expectations that have thus far shaped their lives, and those that are bound to have an impact on their futures. For others, it was simply another step of an ongoing journey toward wholeness. I was gratified to hear several contributors say, "I never really thought about it before. But since you asked, now I can see that . . . " For still others, it was an act of charity performed for the benefit of another person—me, and whoever might read this book. For myself, it was a move toward greater understanding and tolerance. It was also a beginning of an advocacy project I intend to continue.

If nothing else, I'm less naive now than when I commenced this project two years ago. I've contemplated more severe pain and more brilliant happiness, listened to tales of greater failure and bolder triumph than ever before. My hope is that you, the reader, may catch a glimpse of the drama in the lives of the women who have spoken through these pages; that you will see and understand in greater measure.

And I hope that the experience of hearing other women share deeply, with candor and honesty, will inspire you to do likewise.

What are your expectations? Can you be honest with yourself, with your family, with your friends— with God—about your desires for life? Can you hear your own voice on these pages? Was there a woman who expressed your own unspoken thoughts?

Do you feel battered by the expectations of those who influence your life? Is it any clearer to you how you might revise expectations so that they are more reasonable, more constructive, more centered on God's will and less on the will of others or yourself?

Is it also possible that *you* are the source of oppressive, inflated or unrealistic expectations for others? Do you hold up a standard that your children, friends, husband, siblings, co-workers, fellow Christians or neighbors cannot possibly attain? Are you forgiving of their faults, or mostly just critical? Do you find yourself in perpetual wonderment that people are so stupid, careless, incompetent . . . so *flawed*? Do you expect perfection from others? Are you more in tune with their shortcomings than with their pain and struggle? Do you believe that most people do the best they can under the circumstances, or do you side with Mark Twain who concluded that "people are no damn good"?

Over the course of this project, I talked to women who have made a paying profession of telling other women that homemaking is the only valid profession for a woman. I talked to women who bemoan the *Playboy* standard for the perfect American female, yet conform to that standard in nearly every way. I talked to women who worry about the population explosion, yet have five children of their own; and to others who think that everybody should have nice big families, yet find two children "quite enough, thank you." I talked to women who decry materialism while living in suburban splendor. I interviewed ministers' wives who harbor grave secret doubts about God and contempt for the church; and I've spoken to "nominal Christians" who have endured tremendous catastrophe with unshakable faith. I've listened to women whose best friends don't know they've had an abortion, a failed teenage marriage, or an extra-marital affair.

SPEAKING THE TRUTH, IN LOVE

I believe we are facing a crisis of honesty in our relationships and in our churches. Perhaps we think it reflects badly on God to admit failure. Perhaps we feel we're the only ones out of step and struggling. Then again, failure is not accounted for in the Gospel of Success preached in many churches these days—a gospel which claims that God richly blesses those who stand squarely in his will. The unspoken flip-side is: if you *don't* have rich blessings you're messing up somehow.

That's pure bunk, as far as I'm concerned. What does such teaching have to do with obedience to God's will, with dying daily to self? Yet the Gospel of Success pervades in the mass of books and magazine articles blithely expounding all the ways women can and should be better and more perfect in every way, written by people wo do not address their own doubts, pain, fear and failure—much less those of the hapless reader.

As I have been admonished by the contributors to *The Lie of the Good Life* to share honestly in my life and in my writing, I now challenge other writers, speakers, teachers, counselors and ministers reading these paragraphs: approach your work with the knowledge that hurting people on the other end of your advice need understanding, acceptance and sympathy—not exhortation to higher achievement. They need comforting as well as commissioning. We can all use correct answers, we can all use encouragement. But the Gospel of Success must be tempered by the Gospel of Sacrifice.

If I decide—as a writer, as a friend—to project a posture of self-contained competence I must be aware that that same competence can do violence to those I love, and toward whom I have responsibilities. As long as I let others believe I've got it all together (when I don't), then I intimidate them with my perfection. My friends soon tire of being weak and needy in a relationship where I'm always strong and successful. Better to suffer in silence than confide in Superwoman!

Did you notice how many women reported good outcomes when they decided to come clean about their failures and problems? Do you remember Patricia, the woman whose teenager was on drugs, and who decided to seek her church's prayers for him? That wasn't an easy thing to do; she could just as well have kept silent, preserving her dignity. But she chose to disclose, because "healing was more important than discretion."

Likewise Cora, who is in a position of leadership among women. You can imagine how hard it was for her to come to the place where she said, "When I share with other women, or when I'm speaking, I'm totally honest about my humanity and imperfections. And this is being very helpful to people. They have the misconception that my life is perfect, I don't have their struggles. But as I share my struggles and imperfections, they open up to me and they become receptive to God's work and his healing in a way that they wouldn't have been otherwise."

It is good for us to remember that Cora—and many others like her who contributed to this book— have tried it the other way around. They tried presenting their best sides, tried inspiring others with their knowledge and insight. But they came to realize that it is through sharing weakness that we become strong, looking to God—not our own competence—for power.

DeAnn draws from the beatitudes: Blessed are those who mourn, for they shall be comforted. "If you don't ever mourn, you're not a candidate for comfort," is her simple observation.

Let us, then, listen to the voices of these women and learn from those who contributed to this book. Let us strive for greater honesty in our relationships and before God. Let us rejoice with those who rejoice, and mourn with those who mourn; share our joys *and* our sorrows. Let's tell the whole truth, in love. May the healing begin.